Kris Brossett has a passion to see p
dom Citizenship is passion in print. |
and apply some essentials for spiritual maturity, as he faithfully and
graciously guides them in this day-by-day discipleship book. He discusses
sin, grace, sanctification, the church, and walking with God – concisely,
illustratively, practically, and accessibly. Wherever you are in your Christian
journey, this book will give you and other believers both instruction and
inspiration for pursuing likeness to Jesus together. I highly recommend it.

Tony Merida
Pastor, Imago Dei Church, Raleigh, North Carolina

This is a wonderfully accessible and refreshing book. Kris is someone who
truly knows the revolutionary power of all that God has done for us in Christ
and all He has for us in Christ, and that deep, personal experience ensures
his writing is infused with a fresh and invigorating vitality. The truths are
tremendous, the illustrations illuminating, the testimony thrilling and the
gospel explanations gripping.

Steve Timmis
Executive Director, Acts 29 Network

Kris reminds us that Jesus is the only solution to our problems in this daily
easy to read devotional. These daily readings will encourage you deeply in
the basics of the faith and lead you beyond religion to the very person of
Jesus Christ. Do the daily readings, meet with a friend weekly to discuss and
watch yourself grow in the faith!

Brian Dye
Executive Director, Legacy Disciple

The mission of the church is to make disciples. Many desire to obey the
command to make disciples but don't know the first step to take, or simply
lack the confidence to take it. In this book, Pastor Kris has created a great
tool for discipleship for both new beginners and seasoned believers to dive
deeper into their understanding of the essential doctrines of the faith. He
connects eternal truths to real life situations and gives the reader a better
understanding of how to apply them in everyday life. I have had the privilege
of discipling two men from different walks of life using this book and have
seen personally how God used this material for their spiritual growth.

Sergio Garcia
Pastor, Kerusso Grace Church, Houston, Texas

Bite-sized readings, piercing questions, and practical applications flowing from glory of the gospel – that's what you get in *Kingdom Citizenship*. Brossett's writing is honest, hopeful, helpful. Read this book and learn what it means to be a hearer and a doer, a faithful citizen in the Kingdom of our risen Christ, who plays their part in the drama of Redemption.

J. A. Medders
Pastor, Redeemer Church,
Author of *Humble Calvinism*

KINGDOM CITIZENSHIP

KRIS BROSSETT

UNDERSTANDING GOD, HIS PLAN, AND OUR PLACE IN IT

CHRISTIAN
FOCUS

Copyright © Kris Brossett 2019

paperback ISBN 978-1-5271-0410-5
epub ISBN 978-1-5271-0461-7
mobi ISBN 978-1-5271-0462-4

10 9 8 7 6 5 4 3 2 1

Published in 2019
by
Christian Focus Publications Ltd,
Geanies House, Fearn, Ross-shire,
IV20 1TW, Scotland, Great Britain

www.christianfocus.com

Cover design by Rubner Durais

Printed and bound by Bell & Bain, Glasgow

TABLE OF CONTENTS

Chapter 6 WALKING WITH GOD

Appendix

To Veronica, Valerie, and Vincent.
I pray that I point you to Jesus.

ACKNOWLEDGEMENTS

I often speak about the power of community. I'm convinced that God's mission advances through the collective efforts of His people – the Church. This means that no person should work alone. As a united force, we are better together – we are called to one another.

There are many people responsible for this work. The book wouldn't be here without the personal influence, contribution, and generosity of those individuals. If God should use this book to advance His Kingdom, the fruit belongs to them.

I want to thank the many men and women who've invested in my life. As our paths have crossed, you've challenged me and made me better. Thank you, John and Adriana Federoff, Matt Moore, Dan, Lisa Schreiber, Mike Brown, and everyone who walked with me early on.

I want to acknowledge the past members of Refuge LA Church. Our journey together shaped me for a lifetime. I've written this book with many of you in mind. I pray that God would multiply the fruit of our season together.

Kurt and Penny Tuffendsam. Your friendship and partnership in the gospel are unmatched. Thank you both for pushing me to write. Many lessons taught in this book were learned alongside you. Kurt, thank you for giving me your plane ticket to make it possible.

I want to thank Richard Ho for your pointed feedback and Erin Popova for meticulously editing the first draft of this work – your input was priceless.

Thank you, Shaun Garman, for finding me a place to write and Eric and Tara Brown for graciously opening your home so that I could finish the manuscript.

Matthew Davison. You've been a tremendous help in the publishing process. Thank you for all that you do for pastors and churches in hard places.

Jennifer. You make me better. You support me, challenge me, and push me to grow as a follower of Jesus. We've journeyed through the gutters and to the top of mountains together. We've grown tremendously, and we have a blast. I love you.

Finally, I'm overwhelmed by grace. Jesus, you never stop pursuing me. I pray that this book serves to advance your Kingdom. Lord, let it point them to you. The glory is yours alone.

FOREWORD

When God has deeply changed a man's life, and has empowered him to articulate the gospel in a simple and profound manner, we would do well to listen. If you walked by my friend Kris Brossett on the street, you would be surprised to hear that he is a preacher. When you listen to his life story, you might be even more surprised that he is a believer at all. In the same way that the disciples questioned whether or not they could accept Saul who became Paul the apostle, you'd probably wonder about Kris. After spending time with Paul and reading the epistles, there is no doubt that Paul had been with Jesus.

As you read the pages of this book, there is no doubt that you'll discover a man who has spent time with Jesus and whose life has been eternally changed. Kris' life tells the story of the power of God as he is changed by the story of the good news the gospel. In the pages of this book, you will be shocked to hear how God changes hearts – and incredibly encouraged as Kris unpacks the truth in a way that you'll not only understand it, but be able to apply in all areas of your life and community.

Whether you are an individual looking to understand the Christian faith, a family looking for a devotional, a group leader looking for a resource to help the people in your care grow in your understanding of the gospel, or a pastor/leader who has been searching for a discipleship tool for your ministry, *Kingdom Citizenship* is a beneficial tool that helps the Christian (young or old) understand the gospel while developing crucial disciplines to help them stay grounded in the faith.

As I read this book, I was praising God for His work in Kris' life, as well as marveling that I get to call this brother a friend. I'm thankful for Kris' continual encouragement to understand the gospel and live in the deep joy that is found by living in disciplined obedience. As you read this book, may you grow in every area of your life as you discover the power of God to change lives, and the disciplines of the Christian faith that enable us to discover that power.

Dr Jim Applegate
Author of *Engage the Church*

INTRODUCTION

'Although by this time you ought to be teachers, you need
someone to teach you the basic principles of God's revelation
again. You need milk, not solid food.' – Heb. 5:12 CSB

Dear Reader,
Everyone grows up, but maturity is a choice. When a grown-up has the maturity of a toddler, it's sad and pathetic. In the same way, when a follower of Christ refuses to mature, it hurts everyone involved. Sadly, many Christians never develop – and instead remain spiritual infants. When it comes time for a believer to take responsibility to pursue their own growth, they stop growing. There comes the point when a person grows past the stage of being fed by someone else. At this time, you must learn to clean, cook, create a budget, and contribute to society. Those who refuse to grow never experience the blessings of maturity and the joy of serving others.

Even when a believer does choose to actively pursue their spiritual growth, there are still challenges. Some people aren't given the opportunity to mature. Maybe that's you. It's impossible to mature if you've never seen maturity. For some people, there's no mature person to learn from. The world is unfair and may have taken that opportunity away from you. If that's you, Jesus came to rescue you. If you pray, He will lead you into maturity. I have written this book to help you along the way. As you mature, be sure to invest in others. It's your spiritual and moral responsibility.

For others, maturity seems out of reach. Sometimes, those with an appearance of maturity can make it seem unachievable. I hope to give you a fresh understanding. Maturity is attainable. God is with His people, and He will lead you into godliness. I've written this book to help you move towards that goal.

In the many years that I've been a Christian, I've observed two big mistakes. First, there are those who know what they believe but don't live like they believe it. When they refuse to act on their faith, they fail to display the power of God in their life. Next, there are those who have authentic faith but have no idea what the Bible teaches. These individuals end up believing and teaching false things about God. Both of these scenarios result in believers hurting themselves and others.

It's important to learn what the Bible teaches about God and to obey what you learn. If you don't obey God, you'll never know His power; if you don't know who God is, you'll obey a god of your own making. It's for this reason that I've written this book. I hope that you commit to knowing the true God. My second hope is that, once you know God, you'll live boldly for Him in the world. My concern is that you'll grow into maturity as a Christian.

WHO IS THIS BOOK FOR?

This book is for new Christians and seasoned Christians alike. I've written this book to give both groups a pathway to maturity. I've also written this book for those who are interested in Christianity. There are excellent books that do a far better job than mine. However, I believe this book is a substantial contribution.

For new Christians, the content of this book will help you gain an understanding of what it means to be a follower of Christ. I've written so that you will have a basic understanding of what Christians believe and why we believe it. I've based each daily reading on real-life scenarios because faith is active and real. I tried to write in a way that would be understandable to many people. If you don't understand a word or concept, don't be lazy. Look it up in the dictionary or ask someone for help. Remember, maturity is a choice.

For seasoned Christians, I've created a tool to help you share your faith. If you aren't making disciples, you're unfaithful. As Kevin De Young notes, 'The one indispensable requirement for producing godly, mature Christians is godly, mature Christians.' The next generation of Christians needs your investment.

I recognize that it's helpful to have a plan. I also understand that some content is written without actual people in mind. I've written this book for my friends and family; for my homies who never made it out of the hood; and for the future of my community. The Church has the power to change the world when she's faithful to her mission. When you obey God, He'll use you as an instrument of healing.

Finally, I've written this for those who don't know Jesus. I hope that you'll see the power of God in my words. The God whom I write about is living and real. My prayer is that you know Him. If that is your desire, this book is for you. However, you must ask God to reveal Himself to you. If you read this without doing so, you're wasting your time.

HOW TO USE THIS BOOK

If you want to get the most out of this book, you must read it in the format that I've prescribed. If you don't, you'll miss out on the many benefits that are in store for you. I didn't write this book to change your mind; I wrote this book to change your life. For this reason, it's essential to follow the instructions. In fact, following directions is critical to maturity.

1. With Others

Life change happens with the involvement of others. That's why this book is meant to be read with other people. It can be read with one other person or in a group setting. The aim is to have a mature person walk you through the content. In this way, the mature Christian is able to share their own personal experience with you. Many lessons are learned over a lifetime. By having a mature Christian walk with you, you'll have the ability to see how God actually works. This is the model prescribed in the Bible. The message of the Gospel is to be taught by others who have personally experienced God.

2. Daily Commitment

There are five daily readings. Each reading builds on one central idea that covers the entire week. Be sure to read, reflect, and answer the questions for each reading. By doing so, you'll have the opportunity to engage with the content. Take notes, journal, and write down any questions that you may have.

3. Weekly Commitment

Each week, you'll gather with others to discuss what you're learning. In this setting, you get to ask questions and hear from others. Don't be afraid; be honest. Ask real questions, even if they seem awkward. Remember, God is real and powerful; He isn't afraid of your questions. Sometimes, your questions will even grow the person who's leading you. You might ask a question that they've never thought of. In this way, you provide them the opportunity to learn alongside you. This is the beauty of God's design for maturing us. Other times, their experience will increase your understanding of what you are learning.

4. Lifetime Commitment

This book is only an introduction. Each reading gives you a launch-pad to discover the endless truth about God. Explore, learn, and commit to maturing in your faith for the rest of your life. I've organized this book so that you can return to it over time. As you grow in Christ, some of what you will learn will make greater sense in the future. This book will help to equip you for that journey.

5. The Appendix

Finally, I've included a list of resources that will help you grow in the future. When you complete this book, you must implement what you learn. Make sure you read through the appendix, as it gives you tools to put your faith into action.

For the Gospel,
Kris Brossett
3 July 2018

WEEK 1
THE WORLD IS BROKEN
'Jesus is the only solution to our problems.'

'If we find ourselves with a desire that nothing in this world can satisfy, the most probable explanation is that we were made for another world.' – C. S. Lewis[1]

The World is Broken

My earliest memories of my father are filled with visits to the LA County Jail. He was in and out of prison the first half of my life, fueled by a vicious heroin habit. When California passed its Three-Strike Law, he was immediately given two. If he committed another serious offense, he would spend the rest of his life in prison. To avoid this, he decided that begging was safer than burglary. He spent the rest of his life homeless and died of liver failure. I'll never forget walking into the hospital room as they pulled the tubes out of his lifeless body. His arms were abscessed from fresh needle wounds. It was over.

That night, I helped my grandma find a place to stay. During the previous year, she had been living on the streets with my dad and now had nowhere to go. I offered a few solutions, which she stubbornly refused. She enabled my father and had her own set of issues. She asked to be dropped off at a dope house, and I decided not to argue. Two days later, a man was shot in the head, and the police raided the property. That was the last I heard from my grandma. At this point, I don't know if she's dead or alive.

At an early age, I learned how the world is broken and how brokenness has a way of repeating itself. In my life, it resulted in more pain.

---

1. C. S. Lewis, *Mere Christianity* (San Francisco: Harper, 1952, 1980), 136.

I got into a lot of trouble, joined a gang, went to jail, and came inches from death. I was only seventeen years old when my blood stained the sidewalk from a gunshot wound. Last year, I took a short walk at a funeral and stumbled upon the grave of a rival gang member. We had fought in juvenile hall. The only difference between the outcomes of our lives is the grace of God. Many of my friends never make it out.

Death has a way of transforming you. One day I will die and so will my wife and kids. In fact, one of us will suffer the loss of the other. This is the painful reality. Who's to say that your child won't get cancer? Think of the parents who wake up to find the lifeless body of their son, destroyed by shrapnel from a bomb. How do you live every day and not consider these things? Especially when it's evident that humans have no solution.

Before considering the fundamentals of Christianity, it's necessary to reflect on the state of the world – it's broken. Jesus is the only solution to our problems. Without a proper view of the situation, you won't understand the need for Jesus. It's not wise to dismiss the process of honest reflection. It takes pure ignorance, profound selfishness, or denial to refute the brokenness in the world. This place is a mess, and something is tragically wrong with humanity.

BIBLE PASSAGES

- *Jeremiah 17:9 csb* – *'The heart is more deceitful than anything else, and incurable – who can understand it?'*

- *1 John 2:15-17 csb* – *'Do not love the world or the things in the world. If anyone loves the world, the love of the Father is not in him. For everything in the world—the lust of the flesh, the lust of the eyes, and the pride in one's possessions—is not from the Father, but is from the world. And the world with its lust is passing away, but the one who does the will of God remains forever.'*

QUESTIONS FOR REFLECTION

1. The Christian's position is that the world is in a sad and corrupt state. Do you see evidence of this? What do you see?

2. What do you believe is the cause of this sadness and corruption?

3. Does the sorrow and corruption of the world eventually affect everyone or just some people?

PRAYER

God, you created the world. I don't fully understand how everything works, but I want to see clearly. Help me to identify where the world is broken.

'Our insight into the need of redemption will largely depend upon our knowledge of the terrible nature of the power that has entered our being.' – Andrew Murray[1]

You Are Broken

As a rebellious teenager, it was easy to blame my absent father or broken home for my behavior. The effects of my upbringing will always linger. However, if the scars exist as a reminder of where I come from, the breath in my lungs tells me who I am today: I'm a grown man with a family of my own; I'm a member of society with social responsibilities; I have a life to live despite my upbringing. At this point, I can no longer blame my past for current decisions.

In the last section, I discussed the mercy I've received. I don't deserve to be alive, and many of my friends haven't had the same opportunities as me. You'd think I'd cherish every day. Surprisingly, I don't! I struggle with bitterness, anger, and jealousy. I even think I deserve more than I have. I want others to recognize my hard work and notice me – I want the world to know who I am! It's pretty disgusting. It's not always evident; but when it shows up, it hurts other people. I'm still broken.

As a pastor, I have the privilege of counseling married couples. In doing so, I've learned the single issue destroying marriage is pride. Relationships crumble when couples hold onto independence, place unreasonable expectations on one another, or refuse to forgive

---

1. Andrew Murray, *Humility* (Bloomington: Bethany House, 2001), 24.

the other person in times of difficulty. The same thing happens in families, the workplace, and between kids on the playground. Conflict is everywhere. We don't trust each other.

I recently heard of an affair between a man's wife and his best friend. Statistics show that sexual predators are often members of the same family. When I was a gangster, I witnessed close friends turn on each other over rumors. The lure of sex, money and power has led to some of the most disturbing crimes. The tendency in humans is to preserve and protect our own interests, regardless of how it may affect others. For this reason, we can go on living our entire lives without acknowledging the suffering of other people in the world – let alone our own city. To solve these problems, we'd have to become radically selfless and get uncomfortable. I don't want to do that, do you?

As I write this chapter, Houston is underwater from a terrible hurricane. Countless lives are lost, and I have friends impacted by the disaster. The images are powerful and move me to tears. But, will they drive me to action? Probably not! I barely want to tackle the homeless crisis in my own city. I remember the time my friend brought a mentally disturbed man to a bible study at my house. I was angry when I had to clean up his diarrhea off my bathroom floor. I don't ever want to do that again. In fact, I'd rather hang out with people who won't intrude on my comfort. I'm selfish. If you're honest, you're a lot like me.

We all have brokenness. Maybe yours isn't identical to mine, but it's there, and there's no way to measure the magnitude of its damage. The coworker you were rude to might beat his wife when he gets home. That's not your fault, but you might have provoked him. Human decisions are interconnected, and the impact we have is frightening. God has created us with the ability to impact the world. Any misuse or distortion of that impact is catastrophic.

BIBLE PASSAGES

- **Romans 3:10-12** csb – 'There is no one righteous, not even one. There is no one who understands; there is no one who seeks God. All have turned away; all alike have become worthless. There is no one who does what is good, not even one.'

- **Psalm 14:3** *CSB* – *'All have turned away; all alike have become corrupt. There is no one who does good, not even one.'*

QUESTIONS FOR REFLECTION

1. Everyone is broken. Do you believe this statement?

2. Where do you see this statement reflected in your life?

3. Are you selfish? Where does selfishness show up in your life?

PRAYER

God, you created me. I don't fully understand how I work, but I want to see clearly. Help me to see where I am broken.

'As the salt flavors every drop in the Atlantic, so does sin affect every atom of our nature. It is so sadly there, so abundantly there, that if you cannot detect it, you are deceived.' – Charles H. Spurgeon[1]

Your Brokenness Contributes to the World's Brokenness

Growing up, I learned to disguise pain with humor. I guarded my feelings so that I wouldn't get hurt. I considered myself easygoing and didn't let much bother me. When a situation arose, I bypassed my feelings by telling a joke. This didn't work when I became married. Keeping my wife at a distance is impossible. Marriage requires intimacy and vulnerability. You have to risk being hurt.

In the previous reading, we established that people are going to hurt you. If it happens on the playground, it will happen in marriage. When it did, I wasn't prepared for my feelings. I was angry and couldn't control my actions. I wanted to lash out. This never happened before. Did my wife implant rage into my heart? Was it her fault? The answer is, 'No!'

My wife uncovered an area of my heart that was hidden. She triggered an instinct that only came out because she was close enough. By letting my guard down, I opened myself up for pain.

---

1. Charles Spurgeon, *'Honestly Dealing with God.'* Metropolitan Tabernacle, Newington (delivered on June 20th, 1875).

When I was hurt, I wanted to hurt back. I've been working on this behavior ever since.

Initially, I blamed the rage on my upbringing – it's what I witnessed. Over time, this became an excuse. Although nothing warrants sinful rage, my wife hadn't been unfaithful; nor had she lied to me; nor had I caught her looking at another man. I was angry over petty things. I was mad because she didn't prioritize my feelings. I only thought about myself. Sadly, I'm not entirely healed from the wounds of my childhood, and my children will have to carry the relational scars. My behavior has hurt my family. I've brought more pain into the world because I'm selfish. It only took the realities of marriage to help me realize it. My behavior has consequences that I'll never comprehend.

The world is broken because you and I are broken. Maybe you think you would never murder, but it could be that you've never been placed in a situation that could trigger a deadly instinct. I've spent years incarcerated with people who had never imagined they'd commit those crimes. But they did.

Are you responsible for the pain in the world? Partly. Your actions have caused pain. You'll never know how much pain you've caused, because your perspective is limited and you can't really understand fully what the consequences of that action truly were. But, even a little pain goes a long way.

Criticism in elementary school can stick with a person forever. A father's obsession with his work can produce abandonment issues in his children. It can make it hard for them to trust anyone. It can lead to depression and suicide. It can ruin their life. All the while, he thought he was doing well for his family. In reality, he was cutting away at the foundation of every future relationship they'd have.

For some of us, it's no secret that we're responsible for the pain in the world. For others, we need to be exposed. Loneliness was behind my smile, and judgment was at the core of my laughter. I needed my wife to help me realize that I don't trust people. I was hurting inside, but I was also hurting others by being a fraud. How could anyone trust me if they didn't really know me? Who else is wearing a mask?

There's no way to know how much pain we've caused; however, God sees the damage. He knows the brokenness that put us in our situation, and He knows the brokenness that keeps us here. If we make excuses for our actions, we'll never begin to heal, and we'll never stop hurting others. For this reason, we must confront our brokenness head on. To do so, we need to know why we're broken in the first place. We'll discuss this subject in the next reading.

BIBLE PASSAGES

- *Isaiah 24:4-5 CSB* – 'The earth mourns and withers; the world wastes away and withers; the exalted people of the earth waste away. The earth is polluted by its inhabitants, for they have transgressed teachings, overstepped decrees, and broken the permanent covenant.'

- *Luke 8:17 CSB* – 'For nothing is concealed that won't be revealed, and nothing hidden that won't be made known and brought to light.'

QUESTIONS FOR REFLECTION

1. How do you disguise pain?
2. How has the brokenness of others caused you pain?
3. What lasting effects will your brokenness have on others?

PRAYER

God, you created others. I don't fully understand how everything works, but I want to see how my brokenness has hurt others. Please, help me uncover areas in my life where I may be blind.

'Evil is a parasite, not an original thing.' – C. S. Lewis[1]

We're Broken Because of the Fall

I've been fascinated with culture since I was a kid. I love crowded places where I can watch people interact. One of my favorite spots is *The Alley* (a large shopping district in downtown Los Angeles). Thousands of people from all over the world shop here daily. It's known for bargain prices and counterfeit products. For a small amount of cash, you can purchase a complete wardrobe of designer brands. You'll never know they're fake until they fall apart, you discover a missing letter in the logo, or you notice that one pant leg is longer than the other. Needless to say, the products sell. People want to keep up with the latest trends, and it drives an entire industry.

My experience at *The Alley* has taught me a lot about humanity. The people who frequent the shops are from all walks of life. Even though they're different, they share a common experience. They want the most out of life with the least amount of investment. I've noticed the same trend as a pastor. I meet people from all over the world who desire the same things. The corporate executive is driven by the same desire as the gangster. One finds his worth in success, and the other sees it in notoriety. In the end, they both

---

1. C. S. Lewis, *Mere Christianity* (San Francisco: Harper, 1952, 1980), 49, 50.

want to be important, influential, and in control of their life. They've merely had different opportunities.

Brokenness doesn't discriminate: The rich and the poor suffer together. One suffers hunger while the other suffers loneliness. The impoverished child cuddles next to her brother in a hut, while the wealthy celebrity is imprisoned in his mansion. Everyone is trying to avoid it. Some people do drugs, and others pursue success. But, nothing works. There's no protection from pain. Eventually, it all falls apart like the clothes they sell at *The Alley*. It's counterfeit happiness.

Why are we never satisfied? Why does everyone experience pain? Why does it feel like something is out of order in the universe? Because it is!

Everything follows a blueprint. From the moment of conception to the moment of birth, an embryo develops into a baby. Oxygen is readily available for the baby to breathe. Trees provide the oxygen. It all works together. It was designed by God to do so. Since God is the designer of the universe, He alone gets to decide how it functions. Only God possesses true authority. For this reason, humans can never define the purpose of our existence, or the function of our existence, without first consulting God.

Since God created everything, you would think He has something to say about human relationships and societies. If everything else has order, should they not also have order? God does have something to say – and yes, they do!

God created humans to depend on Him, to enjoy Him, and to live in harmony with one another. This means God designed human relationships. In doing so, God gave humans the ability to love. Love is not coerced, forced, or mechanical: It's intimate and requires participation. Love can only be exercised in a relationship with others. For this reason, love is not individualistic or self-serving. It's affectionate and generous. To receive love is deeply satisfying. God created humans to love Him and love others; to be loved by Him; and to be loved by others. If this is so, then why is the world full of so much hatred?

Love is impossible without regulation. Imagine a marriage without loyalty. There'd be no trust. It would communicate that you don't value the relationship. This is the opposite of love. It's competitive and unsatisfying. When boundaries are crossed love falls apart. The world is full of hatred because the boundaries that God created to protect love have been crossed.

When did things fall apart for humans? The Bible refers to this moment as *The Fall*. It happened when our first parents betrayed God. They didn't like His boundaries. They liked their ideas better; so, they disobeyed Him. They disrupted the order of creation. It created a disorder. The Bible names that disorder sin. Sin is the reason humans experience pain.

Instead of depending on God, enjoying Him, and living in harmony with one another, humans deny God, compete with one another, and are lonely. There's no true expression of love, because no one can be trusted. There's no security in the world, since nothing in the world lasts forever. The joy we feel for a moment collapses when someone dies or the economy fails. Sin has ruined everything.

Sin has consequences. In the next reading, we'll discuss the consequence of sin. However, at this point, it's important to note that counterfeit joy can never match the real thing. It may come cheaper, but eventually, it will fall apart.

BIBLE PASSAGES

- *Genesis 2:15-17 csb* – 'The Lord God took the man and placed him in the garden of Eden to work it and watch over it. And the Lord God commanded the man, "You are free to eat from any tree of the garden, but you must not eat from the tree of the knowledge of good and evil, for on the day you eat from it, you will certainly die."'

- *Genesis 3:6 csb* – 'The woman saw that the tree was good for food and delightful to look at, and that it was desirable for obtaining wisdom. So she took some of its fruit and ate it; she also gave some to her husband, who was with her, and he ate it.'

- *Romans 5:12 csb* – 'Therefore, just as sin entered the world through one man, and death through sin, in this way death spread to all people, because all sinned.'

QUESTIONS FOR REFLECTION

1. Identify a situation in the past where you thought something would bring satisfaction, but it failed you.

2. What are you currently looking to for comfort? Do you think it will have different results? Why?

3. How does the fall guarantee that, apart from God, nothing will truly satisfy you forever?

PRAYER

God, you created the world. You are the source of satisfaction. Help me identify the areas in my life where I don't believe this. Help me to trust you.

'Hell is God's great compliment to the reality of human freedom and the dignity of human choice.' – G. K. Chesterton[1]

We're Accountable for the Brokenness We Cause

I never liked playing video games growing up, although, I can see the draw. In a video game, if you mess up, you can hit the reset button and start over. It's not the same in real life. Our decisions have consequences that we can never take back. We can't start over.

We've already discussed how your decisions affect others. Humans are interconnected, and society is impacted by the decisions of people. The sinful choices you make destroy society. You're not the only one who has to suffer the consequences of your actions. Like a rock thrown into still water, every lousy decision sends a ripple effect of pain throughout the world.

I once attended a funeral where the mother of the dead tried to jump into the grave – her screams were felt. Her son was young, funny, and loved. A rival gang kicked down his door and shot him to death. His girlfriend had held him as he died. He's part of the ripple. So is she. His dad, brothers, and cousins were all gangsters. His upbringing guided him towards the lifestyle. Now, he's dead.

He also created a ripple. His girlfriend has to live with the memories forever. The killers were never caught, and the neighbors live in fear.

---

1. Quoted in: Lee Strobel, *A Case for Faith* (Grand Rapids: Zondervan, 2000), 169.

The property value of the complex dropped, and innocent people were—and are—affected. His decisions have consequences that he will never experience.

You and I are unable to comprehend how far the ripple goes. You may think your sin isn't severe, but God sees the full effect. The smallest lie can create a tidal wave that eventually leads to death and destruction. Since you didn't create this world, your sin kills and destroys what belongs to God.

The mother of my friend wants the killers to pay for murdering her son. If you're wronged at work, you expect justice. If you're robbed, you want your property back. Justice affirms our pain. It has a way of mending what is broken. It gives us hope and exposes evil for what it is. Justice is good; God is just.

Some things cannot be fixed with an apology. Even if the killers are caught, her son is gone forever. If stolen property is returned, the trauma of being robbed will never go away. Sin has permanently damaged the world as we know it. How is justice served when no one can repay God for the tidal wave of pain caused by sin? No amount of punishment will ever make right was has been wronged. It's impossible for humans.

This puts every human in a terrifying spot: We have a debt that we cannot pay. The Bible tells us that the punishment for sin is Hell, and we're all on death row. Hell is a place of torment where God's justice will be served, as those who have sinned against Him will be separated from Him for eternity. Since sin offends the Eternal God, the punishment for sin lasts forever. At this point, you should be scared. But God has not left us without hope.

There is a way to satisfy the justice of God: Jesus is the way. In the following chapters, we'll discuss the good news of Jesus and what it means to be one of His followers. We'll learn that Jesus satisfied the just requirements of God's perfect law, and provides hope for a world plagued by sin.

BIBLE PASSAGES

- *James 1:14-15* CSB – *'But each person is tempted when he is drawn away and enticed by his own evil desire. Then after desire has* conceived, it gives birth to sin, and when sin is fully grown, it gives birth to death.'

- **Romans 6:23** csb – 'For the wages of sin is death, but the gift of God is eternal life in Jesus Christ our Lord.'

QUESTIONS FOR REFLECTION

1. Identify a situation where you have required justice from some-one who has wronged you.

2. Think of a situation where 'little' sins can turn into 'tidal waves' of pain. How should God punish 'little' sins?

3. How do you feel about hell, and about God's judgment of sin? Is it loving of God to send people to hell? Are you interested in learning more about Jesus?

PRAYER

God, I have destroyed the world. I have caused others pain. I have caused you pain. Please forgive me and show me how to meet the requirements of your justice.

Reflections

Summary

In a short paragraph, summarize what you've learned in this chapter:

....

....

....

....

....

....

....

....

Questions

Write down any questions you would like to ask at your next meet-up:

....

....

....

....

....

....

....

....

WEEK 2
THE LIE AND THE PROMISE

'Sin entered the world when the first humans believed Satan.'

*'Satan's first device to draw the soul into sin is, to present the
bait – and hide the hook; to present the golden cup – and hide
the poison; to present the sweet, the pleasure, and the profit
that may flow in upon the soul by yielding to sin – and to hide
from the soul the wrath and misery that will certainly follow the
committing of sin.'* – Thomas Brooks[1]

We've Been Deceived

The other day, my son came home with a business card belonging to
the parent of his classmate. She works at a theme park. The boy told
my son it was a free pass – and my son was ready to organize a family
trip with it. The crayon writing on the back revealed the truth: The
kid had lied. My son was confused and upset when I told him. Lying
is destructive.

To believe a lie can be equally painful. Imagine thinking that your
spouse was unfaithful when he or she wasn't. It would destroy the
relationship and hurt you both. It would be a great tragedy; it would
be an offense. Lying seems like one of the smaller sins in comparison
to murder or adultery, but all the sin and suffering in the world began
with a lie.

When God created the world, He created the physical realm, where
we live – but He also created the spiritual realm, where God lives. The
physical realm and the spiritual realm are interconnected. In fact, in

1. Thomas Brooks, *Precious Remedies Against Satan's Devices* (Feather Trail
Press, 2010), 15.

the future, they will become one. In the spiritual realm, God created spiritual beings. These beings are powerful spirits that exist to serve God. He called them angels. Angels are different than humans. The primary purpose of angels is to do God's work; humans were created in the image of God and are referred to as His children. Since angels and humans were designed for different reasons, God's relationship with humans is different than His relationship with angels. There's a difference between a servant and a son. A son enjoys an intimate relationship with his father, while a servant is only a hired hand. A son is honored at his father's house, while a servant is there to serve the family. A son has rights to all that belongs to his father, and a servant does not. In the eyes of God, humans are given a higher place than angels. The lie began with a fallen angel, now referred to as Satan.

There aren't a lot of details about Satan, but we know that he became proud and rebelled against God. He wanted more than he was given and rebelled against God. He led a group of angels to rebel with him. In the previous chapter, we discussed the justice of God. Because God is just, He expelled Satan from His presence and promised to destroy him, along with the angels he led into rebellion.

When God created humans, He placed them in an environment where they could thrive. He gave them meaningful work, creative expression, and He hung out with them. It was an environment built for a relationship between God and humans. To protect the relationship, He set boundaries. By living within these boundaries, humans could enjoy a satisfying relationship with God. The consequence for stepping outside of these boundaries was death. Satan hated humans and wanted us dead.

Sin entered the world, as we know it, when the first humans believed Satan. He told the same lie that got him removed from God's presence. He said, 'God is keeping you from being all that you can be!' He led them to believe that they didn't need God to manage their own lives. The humans believed Satan and wanted more than God had provided. They crossed the line, and all of humanity suffered the consequences. They weren't happy with who God created them to be – and neither are we.

It may seem innocent and playful, but the child who gave my son the card was full of lust and deception. He wanted to be more than he is. He wanted the glory that Satan promised. Tragically, the lie is not true, and we've been deceived. In the next reading, we'll learn how Satan's deception has influenced world thought. We'll see how world religions, and societies, rest on Satan's lie.

BIBLE PASSAGES

- **Genesis 1:26-28** *csb* – *'Then God said, "Let us make man in our image, according to our likeness. They will rule the fish of the sea, the birds of the sky, the livestock, the whole earth, and the creatures that crawl on the earth." So God created man in his own image; he created him in the image of God; he created them male and female. God blessed them, and God said to them, 'Be fruitful, multiply, fill the earth, and subdue it. Rule the fish of the sea, the birds of the sky, and every creature that crawls on the earth.'*

- **Genesis 3:1-6** *csb* – *'Now the serpent was the most cunning of all the wild animals that the Lord God had made. He said to the woman, "Did God really say, 'You can't eat from any tree in the garden'?" The woman said to the serpent, "We may eat the fruit from the trees in the garden. But about the fruit of the tree in the middle of the garden, God said, 'You must not eat it or touch it, or you will die.'" "No! You will not die," the serpent said to the woman. "In fact, God knows that when you eat it your eyes will be opened and you will be like God, knowing good and evil." The woman saw that the tree was good for food and delightful to look at, and that it was desirable for obtaining wisdom. So she took some of its fruit and ate it; she also gave some to her husband, who was with her, and he ate it.'*

QUESTIONS FOR REFLECTION

1. Do you feel like you can figure out how to live your life without God?

2. Can you identify an area in your life where you aren't happy with how God has made you?

3. Did you know that God created you in His image and that He wants to bless you?

PRAYER

Father, you created me. You know what I need, and you love me. I'm sorry for having believed the lie.

'Because the fall of man was occasioned by seeking knowledge, God uses the foolishness of the cross to destroy the wisdom of the wise.' – Watchman Nee[1]

World Religions Rest On Satan's Deception

When my dad promised to quit using heroin, I believed him. Sadly, he never kept his promise. The lies hurt more than the addiction. At one point, I asked for the truth. He finally told me he would never stop. It didn't even bother me; it was the beginning of a real relationship.

Life is difficult when you don't know who to trust. Who wants to be lied to? When it comes to God and the purpose of human existence, it's important to know the truth. This can be confusing in a world that's full of opinions. In my community, an Islamic Center, a Scientology building, and a Buddhist Temple are within walking distance. Mormons and Jehovah's Witnesses flock the streets; while music studios produce the next superstars, promising that success will answer the question of your existence. Who's telling the truth?

If you're not informed, you'll open yourself up to lies. Thankfully, it's not as complicated as it seems. While every religion is different in nature, they are fundamentally the same. In fact, Christianity is the only one that is different. I recognize this is a bold statement, but I

---

1. Watchman Nee, *The Spiritual Man* (Christian Fellowship Publishers), Bk. 1, Ch. 3.

stand by it and encourage you to do the research. Let's take a look at the differences.

Christians believe the world is broken because of sin. Remember, to sin is to accept the lie of Satan. Satan says that humans don't need God. Instead, they can work towards happiness on their own. As you can see, sin is self-centered; it diverts attention away from God and focuses the attention on humans. In this way, sin is destructive. It's destructive because it's a lie. Humans *do* need God because He created humans. When God is rejected, it presents devastating problems.

By nature, humans are greedy, selfish, and abusive. We're full of jealousy and are envious of others. Some people take what they want by force, and themselves and others cripple in shame when they fail. We're slaves to our desires and we destroy the world. Consider the way that sin has affected the society that you're a part of. Everyone is a victim of sin.

Sin doesn't only hurt others; sin offends God. Since He created us, He knows what we need. By ignoring God, we ignore the author of our existence. Our independence leads to destruction because God knows best. When we look at creation, we see that God freely gives. When we learn that God created humans in His image, we don't have to feel shame when our situation makes us feel worthless. As you can see, to reject God is foolish – and the consequences aren't worth the independence.

In Christianity, we acknowledge sin; but the world doesn't. We know that we've destroyed the world – and we're devastated. Christians feel sorrow for sin. It's for this reason that we turn to Jesus.

Although there's no way to fix what we've done, Christians recognize that we must stop offending. We must admit our need for God and turn away from sin. We must acknowledge that humans cannot exist without God, and that [they/we] must turn back to Him. However, even this cannot fix our condition.

Remember, God is just. In this way, He requires a payment for the sin we've committed. He's perfect, and we've destroyed what belongs to Him. But, we don't have enough to repay Him! For this reason, God defeated the satanic lie and accomplished salvation on His own.

Satan said that humans should turn away from God because we don't need Him; he said that God was holding out on us. This was not true in the Garden, and it's not true now. God could have cut His losses and could have left us to suffer the consequence of sin on our own, but He didn't. Instead, He provided the very thing that we needed, and shows that Satan is a liar. God displayed His love for us by sacrificing His own son as a payment for sin.

Jesus became a man, lived a perfect life, and died the death we deserve. He then rose from the grave and defeated the power of sin. Then, like a victorious athlete representing a nation, Jesus places the medal He won on the neck of whoever confesses their sin and calls on His name. This means, if you turn to Jesus, you'll be victorious over sin. If you reject Jesus, you will suffer the consequences of sin on your own. As you can see, humans are in desperate need of Jesus.

Every other religion minimizes sin and elevates man. Buddhists must detach from the world, and Hindus acquire freedom through karma. Mormons work for a heavenly kingdom where their spirit children will worship them. Jehovah's Witnesses and Muslims earn their way to God by their holiness and good works. Atheists work their way to the top. Do you see the pattern? Apart from Christianity, every system revolves around humans. In this way, they're all variations of Satan's lie. If you bring something to the table, you're going to be at risk of looking to your offering to save you. If this train of thought destroyed the world, it's powerless to protect you. Jesus is the only way to freedom.

In the next reading, we'll look more specifically at how God responded to sin. As we develop this idea, we'll gain a more complete understanding of our need for Jesus. If we don't understand the need for Jesus, we'll fail to live an authentic Christian life.

BIBLE PASSAGES

- **John 14:6** csb – *'Jesus told him, "I am the way, the truth, and the life. No one comes to the Father except through me".'*

- **Ephesians 2:4-9** csb – *'But God, who is rich in mercy, because of his great love that he had for us, made us alive with Christ even though* *we were dead in trespasses. You are saved by grace! He also raised us up with him and seated us with him in the heavens in Christ Jesus, so that in the coming ages he might display the immeasurable riches of his grace through his kindness to us in Christ Jesus. For you are saved by grace through faith, and this is not from yourselves; it is God's gift – not from works, so that no one can boast.'*

QUESTIONS FOR REFLECTION

1. Are you committed to knowing the truth?

2. Why can we not elevate man? Why is Jesus the only way to God?

3. Have you ever thought you were better than someone? Have you ever felt shame because you weren't as accomplished as someone else?

PRAYER
Father, my sin has offended you. I don't have what it takes to fix that. Please help me understand my need for Jesus.

'Good is original, independent, and constructive; evil is derivative, dependent, and destructive. To be successful, evil needs what it hijacks from goodness.' – Cornelius Plantinga[1]

God Responded to Humanity's Sinful Betrayal

When my son was four, we went on a family walk. As we approached a driveway, I asked him to stop. Crossing without checking for cars is dangerous. In his most mature voice, he told me that I was wrong. I thought to myself, 'Dude, you're four!' My son has inherited my sinful ways.

In the same way that I desire to protect my son from danger, God prepared humans to defeat sin. When God created humans, He gave them a beautiful place to live and spent time in their presence. When Adam, the man, wanted a companion, God answered his longing and created a beautiful woman, Eve, to be his wife. At this point, there was no reason to doubt God's love.

God even warned Adam and Eve of the consequences of sin. He told them that disobedience would result in death. Remember, He gave them strict boundaries for their own protection. But, sin is delusional. It resembles the pride in my son's heart. Adam and Eve ignored the warning of God and made a dangerous choice. Instead

---

1. Cornelius Plantinga, *Not the Way it's Supposed to Be: A Breviary of Sin* (Grand Rapids: Eerdmans, 1995), 89.

of looking to God, who possessed all knowledge, they believed the lie of Satan and wanted more than what God had already given them. This is foolish, since God is the source of all blessings. As we've learned, their choices had devastating results. Now, we're all infected.

Just like physical features, we inherit our parents' sinful nature. As we grow, we sin like them; and our sin has consequences, too. From the moment we're born, we're destined to die like the rest of humanity. Since death isn't natural, it hurts badly. In the same way that my son has inherited my physical features, he's also inherited my sinful nature. This means that you've also inherited your parents' sinful nature. God knew this was the outcome, and responded immediately.

When sin entered the world, God saw the destruction, hurt, and pain it would cause. He could've destroyed everything. If God did this, it would've been fair and just. Instead, He set into motion a plan to destroy Satan and his lie. He chose to show mercy and rescue His children. However, sin has consequences. If God didn't punish sin, He wouldn't be good, and we shouldn't trust Him. If God allowed evil to remain in the world without responding, He would be evil. But, God does do something about sin. He removes it from His presence and promises to destroy it.

When Satan and the angels sinned, they were cast out of Heaven; when Adam and Eve sinned, they were thrown out of their home. Since God is perfect, He's unable to be in the presence of sin. For this reason, you can't have a relationship with God while actively living in sin. It's become fashionable for people to say they love God while living in rebellion of Him. They're deceived.

When Adam and Eve sinned, shame set in. God knew this would happen, that's why He warned them. Sin produces shame. Imagine betraying your closest friend and most loyal companion. That's what it's like when you betray God. It's the reason every sinner feels like a fraud. To live in disobedience to God is to go against what's natural for humans. To make matters worse, God knew exactly what Adam and Eve had done. They couldn't hide; they were naked and exposed.

At this point, God could've destroyed them. Instead, He covered their shame. God killed an innocent animal and made clothes for

45

them with its skin. In doing this, He painted a picture of redemption. Only innocent blood can pay the cost of sin, and only God can cover shame. This was a symbol of Jesus. As you can see, God responded to humans differently than angels. He provided a pathway of redemption.

Although God cared for the humans, sin still had consequences. God cursed Adam and Eve, and life became difficult. Instead of being full of joy, it became full of tears. This is the human experience: death, sadness, greed, and suffering. Our experience is the result of sin.

During the time God responded to sin, He made a promise. He wasn't going to let Satan's lie ruin His plan for humanity. Instead, He'd use the plan of Satan against him. While Satan believed sin would destroy humanity, God promised deliverance through the very woman whom Satan deceived. Through her offspring, a son would be born, and He would expose the lie of Satan. His birth would be a miracle, because He'd be born of a woman but not of man. He'd be born of God. In this way, God would provide salvation on His own and man could never take credit. Remember, that's what makes Christianity unique. As God promised, a virgin gave birth to Jesus.

When Jesus rose from the grave, Satan's plan collapsed on his head. In Jesus' death, sin was paid for, and redemption became available. Not only does God provide for humans, He does so sacrificially.

On the cross, we see the character of God. First, we see that God loves us. God will go to great lengths to display this love. Next, we see that God doesn't care about human opinions; He'll always accomplish His plan. When the wicked men asked Jesus to come off of the cross and prove that He is God, they were foolish and delusional. He didn't move. For this reason, we must heed the warnings of God. Salvation is available in Jesus alone. He won't change His mind because you protest.

So we see, God responded to sin by sending Jesus. We also know that He made a promise to redeem the world. If this is true, which it is, then we should see evidence of this promise in the world. In the next reading, we'll identify what God has been doing throughout history to fulfill this promise.

BIBLE PASSAGES

- **Genesis 3:14-15** *csb* – *'Because you have done this, you are cursed more than any livestock and more than any wild animal. You will move on your belly and eat dust all the days of your life. I will put hostility between you and the woman, and between your offspring and her offspring. He will strike your head, and you will strike his heel.'*

- **Romans 16:20** *csb* – *'The God of peace will soon crush Satan under your feet. The grace of our Lord Jesus be with you.'*

QUESTIONS FOR REFLECTION

1. If God created you, does He understand your needs?

2. Why is it foolish to disobey God?

3. Should God have destroyed humanity? How does He respond to them?

PRAYER

God, you are loving and merciful. You could have destroyed everyone. Instead, you chose to spare your creation. You love us. Forgive me for accusing you. Thank you, Jesus, for crushing Satan.

'If there is one single molecule in this universe running around loose, totally free of God's sovereignty, then we have no guarantee that a single promise of God will ever be fulfilled.' – R. C. Sproul[1]

God Has Been Working To Redeem Humanity Throughout History

One of my friends is a singer. He was recently nominated for the arrangement of instruments on his new album. When I asked him what this meant, he shared how the timing and placement of instruments matters. If you've ever been to an orchestra, you know what I mean.

Most people don't have an accurate depiction of God or heaven. For example, many believe that God is sitting in heaven with a checklist waiting to punish the naughty and award the nice. However, God isn't Santa Claus. Everyone's evil; therefore, everyone's in danger.

When our assumptions about God are wrong, it leads to sin. For example, people believe that God is silent in the face of evil. In response, they judge God. However, when we look at history, we see that God is actively fulfilling the promise He made in the Garden. He's doing away with suffering and is in complete control of everything. So the question is posed, 'What is God doing?' As we'll see, He's fulfilling His promise perfectly. Everything is arranged.

---

1. R. C. Sproul, *Chosen by God* (Carol Stream: Tyndale House Publishers, 1994), 16.

Salvation is more than escaping Hell; God invites us into His *Kingdom*. The *Kingdom of Heaven* involves the restoration of the Earth and the destruction of sin. This means God will restore Creation to its intended purpose. *Heaven* is a literal place where the redeemed will live with God forever. If you're suffering; if you're weak; if you're carrying the scars of abuse, this is good news. In the *Kingdom of Heaven*, there will be no more racism, violence, and addiction; there will be no more suffering. Right now, God is working towards this plan. This means He isn't silent in the face of pain. By looking at history, we're able to see God at work.

When Adam and Eve sinned, the world progressively deteriorated and corruption filled the planet. As a response to evil, God flooded the earth and wiped out everything. However, we learn that God graciously spared a man named Noah and his family. Even though Noah was sinful, he feared God, and it was counted to him as righteousness. By preserving Noah, God preserved humanity. However, things didn't change.

Years later, the new inhabitants of the earth partnered together in a plan to remove God from their lives. Like the previous generations, they believed the lie of Satan. Remember, the sinful nature of humanity is inherited. For this reason, they decided that they didn't need God. Like Adam and Eve, they believed that they could create their own society with their own rules by working together. They built a giant tower as a symbol of their independence. As you can imagine, it didn't work out. In response, God confused the languages and spread humans throughout the earth. No society can determine its own rules – and last.

God is consistent: When people sin, He will punish them. However, God always provides a pathway to redemption. In the very next story, He calls a man named Abram. He promises to bless the world through him. His family would be a billboard to the world. He gave them rules to follow and instructed them to build a mobile structure where He'd meet with them. Later, this portable structure would be turned into a permanent structure: a Temple. His blessing would be on them, and the world would know that He is God. This was the purpose of the Jewish people. God's call of Abram is a direct response to the Tower of

Babel. God set in motion a plan to redeem the world. Unfortunately, the people had a sin problem, and it got them in trouble with God.

Like Adam and Eve, the children of Abram (Israelites) weren't satisfied. They wanted more. They wanted what the other nations had. When we allow sin to take residence in our desires, it will slowly overtake us. Eventually, the Israelites were conquered by Babylon. Nebuchadnezzar, the king of this nation, destroyed the Temple – and the Israelites were taken away into captivity. However, this did not halt the plan of God. The people still had to worship. As a result, they set up small worship spaces called *synagogues*.

Eventually, the Medo-Persian Empire conquered Babylon, to then be succeeded by Ancient Greece. The Greeks, led by Alexander the Great, spread Greek culture; the Greek language dominated the land. During this time, a group of Israelites rebelled against Greece and succeeded. They set up their own empire. Later, when Rome conquered Greece, a man named Antipater led the Israelite offshoot, and the Romans liked him.

Rome is one of the most powerful nations in history. They dominated the world and built a vast system of roads. Because of Antipater, the Jews were allowed to worship God. Because of the Greeks, everyone spoke the same language. Because of Nebuchadnezzar, synagogues seeded the empire. Jesus came at the most advantageous time in history. It was on these roads, in these synagogues, and by this language that the Gospel became a global movement. The arrangement is a masterpiece. A brief study of church history will tell you what God has been doing since then. But for the sake of this reading, it's sufficient to know that God is active.

So you see, God has been working throughout history, and He's working today. He's fulfilling His plan to redeem the world and destroy the Liar. For this reason, it's important to trust God completely. This means you must reject the lie and believe the truth. In the next reading, we'll discuss the truth about God – He keeps His promises. In this way, you can trust God and turn to Him in obedience.

BIBLE PASSAGES

- **Genesis 12:1-3** CSB – 'The LORD said to Abram: Go out from your land, your relatives, and your father's house to the land that I will show you. I will make you into a great nation, I will bless you, I will make your name great, and you will be a blessing. I will bless those who bless you, I will curse anyone who treats you with contempt, and all the peoples on earth will be blessed through you.'

- **Revelation 21:1-4** CSB – 'Then I saw a new heaven and a new earth; for the first heaven and the first earth had passed away, and the sea was no more. I also saw the holy city, the New Jerusalem, coming down out of heaven from God, prepared like a bride adorned for her husband. Then I heard a loud voice from the throne: Look, God's dwelling is with humanity, and he will live with them. They will be his peoples, and God himself will be with them and will be their God. He will wipe away every tear from their eyes. Death will be no more; grief, crying, and pain will be no more, because the previous things have passed away.'

QUESTIONS FOR REFLECTION

1. Many people believe that God is distant. Is He?

2. Do you live like God isn't paying attention?

3. If God has been strategically working throughout history, how should that change your interactions with Him?

PRAYER

Almighty God, you are powerful and wise. You see and work in everything. Help me to submit to your plans. Thank you for working in my life.

'The fear: If I obey God, I will not be happy. This is the same lie that Satan told in the garden.' – Tim Keller[1]

God is Unlike the Liar and Keeps His Promises

I have a hard time trusting people. I wish I had more examples of loyalty and faithfulness, but I don't. I know loyal and faithful people exist; however, it always seems like someone has an angle. I've witnessed great betrayal happen between members of the same family. When the people you trust betray you, it can influence your view of God. For example, I struggle with believing that God will keep His promises when my earthly father broke his. Since I don't know what it's like to have a loving father, I struggle to relate to God in that way. Thankfully, God is not like humans: He has integrity. He said that Eve's offspring would crush the head of Satan, and He did. Jesus defeated the lie.

Remember, Satan said that God is unreliable and untrustworthy. Now that we know that Adam and Eve believed him and rebelled, we understand why we can't trust people. We know what's inside of them. People are fickle. This is the reason we lock our doors and have armies. We're suspicious of everyone. At times, we can become suspicious of God. But God has given us no reason to be wary of Him. He's kept every promise He's ever made.

1. Tim Keller (@timkellernyc), 'The fear: If I obey God, I will not be happy. This is the...,' Twitter post, November 16th, 2015, https://twitter.com/timkellernyc/status/666352852793753600/.

I can only imagine what Satan thought when Eve ate the fruit. He knew that humans couldn't repair what they had broken – the cost was too high. At this point, he would expect God to destroy them. Since sin brought death into the world, Adam and Eve deserved to die. Did God place them in a circumstance that was too heavy and unfair? Satan would lead you to believe that He did. However, Satan is a liar. God did the very opposite. Let's consider what God did in response.

God, the Son, became a man. Jesus lived the life that Adam should have lived and pleased God. Then, He did the unimaginable: He took His perfect life and gave it away. Jesus went to the cross as a sinless man. In doing so, He became the only sacrifice that could pay for sin. After going into the grave, Jesus defeated death. In His resurrection, He broke the curse of sin. In doing so, humans no longer had to be enslaved to sin. In Christ, you don't have to be controlled by sin any longer. This means, you can begin to heal now and stop hurting others. It means there's hope for the world in Jesus.

Jesus defeated sin and death by His death and resurrection and went to heaven to be with the Father. He received all of the honor and glory that belongs to Him and He provided redemption to whoever calls on His name. The Bible tells us that Jesus literally stands in the place of sinners, and pleads their case to the Father. This means, if you are a Christian, when God sees you, He sees His perfect Son. This is what it means when it says Jesus covers you in His blood. The blood of Jesus covers believers and makes them pure. In this way, God will accept everyone who calls on the name of Jesus as sons and daughters. His blood covers their sins, and their sinful life is traded for His perfect one. Why would we ever believe that God didn't love us when He sacrificed His own son for sinners like you and me?

If you doubt that God loves you, you're deceived. There isn't a reason in the world to question God's love for you. He kept His promise to Eve, and He'll keep His promise to you. God keeps His promises: He'll return to judge the living and the dead; He'll do away with sin and suffering; He'll bring forth His Kingdom. You must turn to Jesus. If you reject Him, the curse of sin remains on your life, and the consequence of sin stays.

Every lie is defeated by the truth. Satan's lie says that humans can exist apart from God – that's untrue. Humans depend on God for everything. Just as Satan's lie brought death into the world, the truth brings life. For this reason, salvation is through Jesus alone. You must declare your need for Jesus to be saved from the consequence of sin. You brought nothing into this world, and you can't protect yourself. However, God provided what you need, but did not earn, in Jesus. This is *grace*.

In this chapter, we've learned why the world is the way that it is. We've also learned about what God has done in response. In the next chapter, we're going to dive deeper into the subject of *grace*. *Grace* is at the center of the Christian message. We're going to learn the definition of *grace*, and learn how it changes everything.

BIBLE PASSAGES

- *John 8:44 csb* – *'You are of your father the devil, and you want to carry out your father's desires. He was a murderer from the beginning and does not stand in the truth, because there is no truth in him. When he tells a lie, he speaks from his own nature, because he is a liar and the father of lies.'*

- *John 6:63 csb* – *'The Spirit is the one who gives life. The flesh doesn't help at all. The words that I have spoken to you are spirit and are life.'*

- *Matthew 11:28-30 csb* – *'Come to me, all of you who are weary and burdened, and I will give you rest. Take up my yoke and learn from me, because I am lowly and humble in heart, and you will find rest for your souls. For my yoke is easy and my burden is light.'*

QUESTIONS FOR REFLECTION

1. If you're honest, where are you struggling to trust God?

2. From what you have learned, is God trustworthy?

3. Do you still believe the lie? Have you turned to Jesus and turned away from your sin?

PRAYER
Jesus, I need you. I cannot please God on my own. Please forgive me; I am nothing without you!

Reflections

Summary

In a short paragraph, summarize what you've learned in this chapter:

....

....

....

....

....

....

....

....

Questions

Write down any questions you would like to ask at your next meet-up:

....

....

....

....

....

....

....

....

Summary

In a short paragraph, summarize what you've learned in this chapter.

Questions

Write down any question you would like to ask at your next meeting.

WEEK 3
GOD IS GRACIOUS

*'If we ever doubt God's desire to bless
humanity, we only need to look at Jesus.'*

'Grace means undeserved kindness. It is the gift of God to man the moment he sees he is unworthy of God's favor.' – D. L. Moody[1]

Grace is Good News

Teenagers are brutally honest and foolishly vulnerable. My daughter recently entered the sixth grade, and I'm saddened by her experience. I've witnessed the sweetest kids grow into victims and abusers. Teenagers betray friends for popularity, abuse weaker students, and rebel against authority. Many of the kids are driven by insecurity. They're terrified of judgment and will do anything to avoid it. Deep emotional scars originate in middle school. Teenagers want to be *glorious*.

What is glory? Glory is magnificence. To be glorious is to be worthy of worship – only God is glorious. The teenage desire for glory is part of the human desire to be God. In the last chapter, we learned that Adam and Eve wanted to be God. Teenagers want to be God, and so do adults.

The desire for glory doesn't look the same in everyone. For example, not all people want to be famous – some people hide from the public eye because they're terrified of failure. If they're recognized, they believe they'll be rejected. Other people love attention and will do anything for praise. Both are driven by the desire for glory. While one is afraid of looking less magnificent, the other wants you to know

---

1. Dwight L. Moody, *Moody's Anecdotes and Illustrations,* ed. Rev. J. B. McClure (Harrington: Delmarva Publications, 2014).

how brilliant they are. Either way, both individuals care about how others view them. This is a heavy burden to carry.

It's an amazing thing that humans are created in the image of God. It means that we already possess a measure of magnificence. The world doesn't get to define who we are. God does, and He says that we're magnificent because He made us so. On top of that, He promises to provide all that we need – God promises to bless us. Since He's the creator of everything, He has the power to bless us; He also has the wisdom to know what we need.

If we ever doubt God's desire to bless us, we only need to look at Jesus. God sent Jesus into the world to pay the penalty for the pain that our sin has caused. We've learned that our sin separates us from the Father. Jesus paid the penalty for sin through His own suffering. Since our sin separates us from God—eliminating blessing—the sacrifice of Jesus makes blessing possible. God is the source of all blessing. This means God sacrificed His Son so that He can bless us. We should never doubt God's love, and we must turn to Jesus – not only to experience God's blessings, but also to accept God's gracious pardon of our sins.

Grace is favor that you don't deserve. Favor can be defined as approval, kindness, or support. Out of His loving kindness, God promises to support and approve those who turn from their sin and trust in Jesus. We know that we can do nothing to earn God's favor. This means that God shows us favor in spite of our wickedness – only because of Jesus. This means, the kids in my daughter's school don't have to live for the approval of others. Neither do we. If we trust in Jesus, God approves of us. Since He does so by grace, we don't have to chase after glory. In this way, you can be free from the opinions of others and live the life God has set before you. For this reason, *grace* is good news. If God sent His Son to die a painful death as a penalty for sin so that you can experience the blessing of salvation, you can be sure that He'll provide everything you need.

Imagine a world that's controlled by grace. What if we never felt jealousy again? What if we were thankful for the things we have, and stopped complaining? Marriages would be healed, and the poor wouldn't be oppressed. Grace changes everything.

Because of grace, we can be honest about who we are. We don't have to make excuses for sin – because Jesus provides forgiveness. When we stop making excuses, others can heal – and so can we. Imagine a society where people stopped making excuses for sin. Many problems never get fixed because we refuse to admit that they exist. There's no reason to minimize sin when Jesus stands in our place.

By God's grace, we can be all that He's created us to be. We can't be anything, but we don't need that ability. Grace allows us to love others, be satisfied with who we are, and be a blessing to the world. Grace is good news. In the next reading, we'll learn how grace has the ability to change the world.

BIBLE PASSAGES

- **Ephesians 2:8-9** *CSB* – *'For you are saved by grace through faith, and this is not from yourselves; it is God's gift – not from works, so that no one can boast.'*
- **1 John 4:9-11** *CSB* – *'God's love was revealed among us in this way: God sent his one and only Son into the world so that we might live through him. Love consists in this: not that we loved God, but that he loved us and sent his Son to be the atoning sacrifice for our sins. Dear friends, if God loved us in this way, we also must love one another.'*

QUESTIONS FOR REFLECTION

1. Where do you see the desire for glory in your own life? Do you look for attention or hide from the public eye? Are you exhausted?
2. Do people know the real you? Are you pursuing a particular life-style because you think it will make your life meaningful?
3. Do you feel free in knowing that God has a plan for your life? If God provided His own son Jesus as a sacrifice for sin, can you trust Him?

PRAYER
God, help me to stop competing with you. Father, thank you for the confidence you give to those who put their trust in you. Thank you for grace.

'When God empowers you to treat others as He treats you, there's not a single part of your life that escapes the impact of the gospel.' – Ken Sande[1]

Grace Changes the World

Before starting a church, I worked in commercial construction. In construction, the contract is the most important document on the job. It details the work you'll do, how long it will take, and the penalties for breaking the contract. Contracts must exist, but it's sad they do. Contracts protect clients and contractors from one another. However, they don't always work. For example, a contractor can fail to note a problem in the building plans if he knows that he can charge more to correct it once it's complete. You'd be surprised to learn how many jobs end up in a courthouse.

Another contract is the United States Constitution. It was created to protect the American people and is the highest form of law in the land. But like any other contract, it gets manipulated and people get hurt. In other countries where protective measures aren't taken, evil goes unchecked, and people are openly oppressed. So we see, social contracts are helpful, but people are evil and find ways to do as they please. For this reason, contracts will never heal the world. What will heal the world?

Looking back, we see that God promised to defeat Satan. We also know that He promised to redeem humanity. Both of these promises

---

1. Ken Sande, *Resolving Everyday Conflict* (Grand Rapids: Baker Books, 2011), 31.

are fulfilled in Jesus. When God cursed Eve, He said that her seed would crush the head of Satan. When He spoke to Abram, God said that his offspring would bless all the families of the earth. Jesus is the seed of Eve and the offspring of Abram. In His death, He paid for sin; and in His resurrection, He defeated its power. Therefore, all who call upon the name of Jesus will be forgiven. In this way, He defeated Satan—who wanted to destroy humanity—by making salvation available to all through His *grace*.

In the last reading, we learned that grace transforms an individual; it also changes a society. When groups of people experience the grace of God, they become healers. Instead of hurting others, they begin to bless them; and instead of competing with one another, they love others.

In America, we've learned that no amount of laws can eliminate racism or erase poverty. However, the grace of God has the ability. You can't look down on others when you deserve punishment for sin, and you can't remain silent in the face of suffering when Jesus did the opposite for you. When grace enters a man, he becomes an instrument of grace. When he's unleashed into society, society itself begins to heal. This is God's intention for His people.

We long for the day when Jesus will return and do away with suffering; but Christians are a preview of what's to come. The Church is an instrument of mercy to a dying world. God commands that we comfort the hurting, serve the poor, stand against injustice, and bless others. Christians are called to generosity, mercy, sacrifice, and love. Historically, Christians have been known to give their lives on behalf of others. They do so willingly because of the *grace* of our Lord Jesus.

So we see, as grace transforms an individual, it has the power to change the world. Next, we'll look at the specific way transformation happens to a person who experiences the grace of our Lord Jesus. The person who isn't transformed by grace fails to represent God in the world. In fact, a person who isn't transformed by grace doesn't know Jesus at all.

BIBLE PASSAGES

- ***Titus 2:11-14*** csb – *'For the grace of God has appeared, bringing salvation for all people, instructing us to deny godlessness and* *worldly lusts and to live in a sensible, righteous, and godly way in the present age, while we wait for the blessed hope, the appearing of the glory of our great God and Savior, Jesus Christ. He gave himself for us to redeem us from all lawlessness and to cleanse for himself a people for his own possession, eager to do good works.'*

- **Galatians 3:27-29** csb – *'For those of you who were baptized into Christ have been clothed with Christ. There is no Jew or Greek, slave or free, male and female; since you are all one in Christ Jesus. And if you belong to Christ, then you are Abraham's seed, heirs according to the promise.'*

QUESTIONS FOR REFLECTION

1. Laws exist to protect people from one another. Why do we need protection?

2. Has any law eliminated our need for protection from others? If not, how can we be sure that others won't manipulate the law to hurt people?

3. When a person encounters the grace of God, they are transformed by this grace. How does grace impact society?

PRAYER
Jesus, thank you for offering your life as a sacrifice for sin. I cannot change my own heart. Please transform me by your grace so that I may be good news to the world.

'Repentance will not make you see Christ, but to see Christ will give you repentance.' – Charles Spurgeon[1]

Grace Leads to Repentance

I learned many valuable lessons as a construction worker. In fact, construction prepared me for life and ministry. A specific lesson comes to mind when I think about grace. It happened when I blatantly disobeyed authority and broke the rules. I should have been fired, but a gracious safety inspector taught me a lesson that I'll never forget.

I was working at a high-profile science lab where strict safety rules were enforced. The inspector on the job had a severe reputation for putting people out of work. If you broke the rules, you lost your job – there were no second chances. For some reason, on this day, he was different.

I had to move a rack of material across a large opening in the ground. To do so, I needed to use a forklift. Barricades surrounded the opening to protect people from falling. To move the material, we had to remove the barricades. The inspector granted us permission but required that we wear safety harnesses. The harnesses were far away; so as soon as he left, we removed the barricade and proceeded to move the material. Unfortunately, the forklift driver jerked the controls and dropped everything. When the material hit the ground, it made a loud noise, and the inspector returned. I feared the worst.

---

1. Quoted in: Stephen McCaskell, *Through the Eyes of Spurgeon* (Brenham: Lucid Books, 2012), 157.

He looked at me with anger and then walked directly into my foreman's office. I followed behind him. When we arrived, he began to scream. Now, standing in the office, I had to give an answer, and I had nothing to say. I was faced with a choice: I could try and explain myself or tell the truth. I decided to tell the truth.

I didn't wear the harness because I was lazy. He should have fired me. However, at the very moment I confessed, his anger disappeared. He lowered his tone, and voiced his concern for me. In his many years on the job, he knew of men who came to work and didn't go home. Laziness could have cost me my life. Instead of firing me, he asked me never to do it again. I didn't.

The grace of this man changed my heart, not his anger. I had put my life in jeopardy, and he wanted to protect me. He had every reason to fire me, but he didn't. Although he wasn't a Christian, his response was very godly. Christians don't stop sinning because we're afraid; we stop sinning because God is gracious and merciful when He should punish us. If we confess our sins before God, He's faithful to forgive us. It's the kindness of God that leads to trust and obedience. Obedience is an essential characteristic in every follower of Jesus.

Consider the kindness of God. He's patient with those who reject Him, and He offered His own Son as a sacrifice for sin. After trusting Jesus, we continue to rebel, and He doesn't stop loving us. Instead, He shows us honor and favor. He even invites us to participate in His plan to redeem the world. No one is as kind as God.

The longer I follow Jesus, I realize how deeply sinful I am. I take for granted the blessings I receive, I complain, and I look down on people who aren't like me. Still, God remains kind; and He's always patient with me. My motivation for following God is birthed out of this love.

Many people view God as I initially regarded the safety inspector. Their motivation to stop sinning is birthed out of their fear of punishment. However, if your motivation for obedience is to avoid the consequences of getting caught, you're missing the point of obedience. Christian obedience is motivated by love.

To follow Jesus, you must turn away from sin; this is called repentance. As a Christian, you can't continue to live however you desire. Remember, sin is destructive to everyone involved. Christians turn away from sin, because they trust God and know that He loves them. The grace of God leads to repentance.

In the next reading, we'll discuss obedience. Repentance and obedience go hand in hand. Both repentance and obedience are regular occurrences in the life of a Christian. However, if not motivated by grace, they can become a scale by which we judge our standing before God. This is never okay. God accepts Christians solely on the basis of what Jesus has accomplished for them. In fact, as we draw near to Jesus, the natural response is to obey Him out of love.

BIBLE PASSAGES

- **Psalm 130:3-4** csb – *'Lord, if you kept an account of iniquities, Lord, who could stand? But with you there is forgiveness, so that you may be revered.'*

- **Romans 2:3-4** csb – *'Do you really think—any one of you who judges those who do such things yet do the same—that you will escape God's judgment? Or do you despise the riches of his kindness, restraint, and patience, not recognizing that God's kindness is intended to lead you to repentance?'*

QUESTIONS FOR REFLECTION

1. Are you driven by fear? Do you feel shame because of your sin? Do you hide sin because you are afraid of being found out?

2. God doesn't accept you because you stopped sinning; He accepts you because of the finished work of Jesus. This means, if you're in Christ, you're forgiven by His grace. How does this make you feel?

3. How does grace change an individual's motives?

PRAYER

Lord, help me to be driven by grace. Hiding sin is exhausting. I want to follow you because you are good and gracious.

WEEK 3 : DAY 4

'With each of us, if we are to have that assurance of forgiveness and restored moral innocence, the fire of God's grace must touch us. It is only through the depths of the forgiving love of God that men and women can be so restored and made ready to serve Him.' – A. W. Tozer[1]

Grace Leads to Obedience

Remember the story of my musician friend? In the reading, we discussed the importance of instrument arrangement on his album. When each instrument is played according to the order it was arranged, it's beautiful. If there's a disruption in the order, the song is ruined. Imagine a musician veering away from the chart in the middle of an orchestra. It'd be disruptive and disrespectful. The audience, composer, and other musicians would suffer the consequences.

Remember, there's order in creation. God has arranged everything according to His purpose and plan. Trees produce oxygen for humans to breathe; the sun is perfectly positioned to support life on the earth, and the moon reflects its light. When men and women come together, children are born as an expression of their love.

God has shared His plan for humanity in the Bible. He's written a beautiful symphony, and we each have an instrument to play. For this reason, it's vital that we play the exact notes we see on the chart without venturing off into a solo. When we follow the pages of Scripture, we play a beautiful song that's rewarding to us and is

---

1. A. W. Tozer, *Worship* (Chicago: Moody, 2017), Ch. 7.

enjoyable to those who listen. When you disrupt the order of creation, it creates disorder in the world. In order to avoid contributing to the disorder in the world, we have to recognize our sin and to commit to obeying God's commands.

Repentance and obedience go together; we don't stop sinning without beginning to obey. Thankfully, God didn't leave us alone to figure it out. Instead, He gave us His Word so that we know precisely what it means to follow Him. This means we don't get to pick and choose what we want to obey. If we don't like something, we have to deny ourselves and submit to God. Remember, Satan convinced the first humans that they didn't need God to figure out how to live. Therefore, if you pick and choose what you want to obey, you still believe this lie.

We must obey God's laws, but we must also obey them for the right reasons. Many believe that obedience earns God's grace; others think that obeying God will cause Him to love you. This is false. In previous readings, we learned that no amount of obedience could please God. God doesn't accept us because we perform for Him; He accepts us because of Jesus. The Christian motivation for obedience comes from the Christian's love for Jesus. In fact, Jesus said that those who love Him would obey Him. We see in the Bible that obedience is motivated by love, and not as a means of earning God's acceptance.

In some Christian circles, this is backward. They pervert obedience by presenting it as a staircase to God. Have you ever thought of obedience in this way? There's a problem with this thinking: a staircase has different levels. If obedience is a staircase, it's only natural that we look down on those below us, and up at those ahead. However, Christians can't look down on anyone – because salvation is in Jesus alone. For this reason, any form of classism is sinful. We can never assume that those ahead are actually ahead. Sin is crafty and deceitful. Jesus says that the last will be first and the first will be last. In the Kingdom of God, there's no room for pride. Therefore, since obedience doesn't earn God's favor, we should only be motivated by love. We see the love of God in Jesus. It's in this way that *grace motivates obedience.*

We obey God because of our love for Him, but we also must recognize that obedience is good for us because God knows what is good for us. When we obey God, we do experience His blessing. Not because we've earned it, but because His ways are right. He knows what we need and why we need it. He wrote the symphony. We might not always agree with Him, but our trust and love lead us to obey.

We don't obey God because we understand His ways; we obey Him because He is God and we are not. If we could understand all the ways of God, we would be Him; and if we need to understand God before we obey Him, we don't follow God. Satan is the one that promised to give us understanding. God promises to be with us.

As Christians repent of sin and trust God in obedience, they begin to transform. This happens to those who experience the grace of God. In the next reading, we'll look at this in the context of your life.

BIBLE PASSAGES

- **Ezekiel 36:26-27** csb – 'I will give you a new heart and put a new spirit within you; I will remove your heart of stone and give you a heart of flesh. I will place my Spirit within you and cause you to follow my statutes and carefully observe my ordinance.'

- **John 14:15** csb – 'If you love me, you will keep my commands.'

QUESTIONS FOR REFLECTION

1. Do you believe that God's order for things is good? If so, do you obey God no matter how difficult it may appear?

2. What should motivate obedience? What's the difference between being driven by fear and being motivated by grace?

3. Why should we obey God even if society says His ways are silly and outdated?

PRAYER

God, sometimes it's hard to trust you. Help me to obey you, knowing that you created everything and will provide all that I need. Help me to obey you even when it's confusing and scary.

WEEK 3 : DAY 5

*'People do not know where they are, they do not know where
they have been, they do not know why they are here, they
do not know where they are going; and they do the whole
thing on borrowed time, borrowed money, borrowed thinking,
and then die. Science may be able to keep you alive so that
you have longer to think it over, but it will never give you any
answer for the purpose of your life.'* – A. W. Tozer[1]

Grace is the Gift of God

Imagine finding a dusty letter in the basement of your grandma's house. As you move across the pages, you learn new things about your family. Questions are answered, and you realize why things are the way they are. There are new insights and a fresh perspective. As you come to the close of the letter, you notice it's addressed to you. At this point, the future of your family becomes very personal.

Friend, you're not reading this by chance. By now, you see that God is very strategic. This book is in your hands because He wants it to be. God is calling you to Himself. He took the time to orchestrate each event in your life and now you're here. He worked in Nebuchadnezzar, Alexander the Great, Antipater, and now you. There are no coincidences.

When I look at my life, all of the dots connect. I started writing poetry at seven and wrote music that told stories and developed

1. A. W. Tozer, *The Purpose of Man,* ed. James L. Snyder (Bloomington: Bethany House Publishers, 2009), 12, 13.

concepts. I learned to communicate my pain through words. I had no idea that God was preparing me to preach. When I taught my first sermon, I had close to twenty years of communication experience. God was active the entire time.

The Scriptures teach that no one comes to God on his own. Remember, salvation is by grace alone because of Jesus alone. It's entirely grace because it begins with God. Satan promised that we could work our way to success and happiness; the Bible teaches that satisfaction is found in God alone. For this reason, Christianity is not just a moral philosophy of living. Instead, it's built upon the blood of a dying Savior who's reaching out to you today. You must reject Satan's lie.

If you're a lifelong Christian, He's calling you to greater faithfulness. If you've recently met Jesus, welcome to the family, I've written this to prepare you. If you're not a Christian, you have the opportunity to turn to Jesus now. If you don't, this book will witness against you when God judges the world of sin.

For those who've been Christians for many years, give it all you've got. Live in obedience to God's Word, make disciples, and finish well. If you're doing so, thank you! If not, will you repent of sin today? God is calling you to complete obedience and worship. If you've had a difficult time, don't stop trusting Him. The same God who brought the Israelites out of Egypt led them through the wilderness. Trust God.

If you've recently begun to follow Jesus, I commend you for committing to the process of maturity. As we continue, we'll learn about living a life of faithfulness. The previous chapters have built the foundation for what you'll learn ahead. Live in obedience to God's Word, make disciples, and finish well. The same God who saved you is faithful to see you to the end. Be courageous and bold.

If you're not a Christian, I'm honored that you would read this far. The following chapters are written for those who want to follow Jesus. They detail what it means to live for Christ over the course of a lifetime. They talk about the process that God uses to transform His people, the purpose of His Church, and what it means to walk with God on a daily basis. If you desire to follow Jesus, you can do so now. The Bible says, 'If you confess with your mouth, "Jesus is Lord," and believe in your heart that God raised Him from the dead, you will be saved' (Rom. 10:9).

The next step is to 'Repent and be baptized ... in the name of Jesus Christ for the forgiveness of your sins, and you will receive the gift of the Holy Spirit' (Acts 2:38 csb). The Holy Spirit is your guarantee. He leads you into all truth, helps you in your weakness, and empowers you to serve God. He's the same Spirit that brought you to this place. God's grace is a gift, and it's offered to you now.

In the next chapter, we'll look at the process that God uses to transform His children. If you're in Christ, God is doing a great work in your life. Keep reading and discover this great work. If you're not a Christian, don't stop reading. Maybe, your experience with Christians has made you suspicious. Perhaps, the following chapters will change your mind.

BIBLE PASSAGES

- **John 6:44** *csb* – *'No one can come to me unless the Father who sent Me draws him, and I will raise him up on the last day.'*

- **Ephesians 2:8** *csb* – *'For you are saved by grace through faith, and this is not from yourselves; it is God's gift.'*

QUESTIONS FOR REFLECTION

1. Have you trusted in Jesus for salvation? If so, are you living in obedience by faith?

2. If you're not a follower of Christ, or if you aren't living faithfully, what's stopping you from turning to Jesus today? Have you written down what you're feeling?

3. Are there any fears that you have yet to share? Do you have doubts that you're afraid to talk about? What are they? There is nothing that God cannot handle; He is full of wisdom and power.

PRAYER

There is no one like you, Jesus. Salvation belongs to you alone. Help me to know you personally and not just know about you. A real God can be known, and you are true.

Summary

In a short paragraph, summarize what you've learned in this chapter:

....

....

....

....

....

....

....

....

Questions

Write down any questions you would like to ask at your next meet-up:

....

....

....

....

....

....

....

....

Summary

In this short paragraph, summarize what you've learned in this chapter.

Questions

Write down any questions you'd like to ask at your next meet-up.

WEEK 4

SANCTIFICATION

'In sanctification, God strips away the sinful habits and patterns that we bring into our relationship with Him from a life of sin.'

'In every case where Jesus meets a religious person and a sexual outcast (as in Luke 7) or a religious person and a racial outcast (as in John 3-4) or a religious person and a political outcast (as in Luke 19), the outcast is the one who connects with Jesus and the elder-brother type does not. Jesus says to the respectable religious leaders "the tax collectors and the prostitutes enter the kingdom before you" (Matt. 21:31).' – Tim Keller[1]

We All Come With Baggage

California recently passed a law to release thousands of inmates. The prisons are overpopulated, and the state can't afford to foot the bill. As a result, those convicted of non-violent crimes will have their sentences reduced. Others, serving a life sentence, are now eligible for parole. Finally, after many years of incarceration, freedom awaits them. I personally know a handful of people that have been released on behalf of this law. The experience they share can teach us about *sanctification* in the Christian life.

Sanctification is the process of renewal that every Christian enters after receiving Jesus. In sanctification, God strips away the sinful habits and patterns that we bring into our relationship with Him from a life of sin. This process confuses many people. They assume that everything changes on the day of their salvation. When stressful situations arise, they immediately panic and even doubt God. Sometimes, they begin to question their salvation and wonder

---

1. Tim Keller, *The Prodigal God* (New York: Penguin Group, 2008), 15.

where they went wrong. They either underestimate the process of sanctification or are entirely unaware of it.

For others, sanctification is confused with *justification*. In *justification*, a person is declared righteous. In Christianity, justification happens at the moment of your salvation. In this way, everything does change on the day you're saved. You're no longer a slave to sin, the penalty for sin has been paid on your behalf, and God accepts you because of Jesus. You're justified in Christ and declared righteous because of Him. However, the smell of your past is still on your clothes. In this way, *justification* is immediate and happens once, while *sanctification* is progressive and occurs for the rest of your life.

Consider the lifer who was just released from prison. After spending twenty years incarcerated, he's now a free man. On the day of his release, his legal status has changed. Instead of being a prisoner of the state, he's now a member of society like the rest of us. He must get a job, pay his taxes, and learn how to cook for himself. There's no one telling him when to wake up, when to eat, or when he's allowed to visit his family. Because he's free, he can now make those decisions on his own. However, because he spent twenty years behind bars, he doesn't have the skills to do so. In fact, he's at a severe disadvantage and learning will be an uphill battle. Over time, he'll learn the skills he needs as he transforms in his thinking and gains the proper experience and training. Sanctification is similar to this process.

Sanctification is difficult. It's hard to admit that we don't have it together when our culture celebrates those who do. The truth is, similar to the prisoner, we all show up with baggage from our past. We may not have the same baggage as others, but there's not a single person without the smell of sin on their clothes. Everyone is saved by grace alone. For this reason, we can be honest with our baggage, and the Lord, through the process of sanctification, will empty our suitcase one shirt at a time. He'll show us how to follow Him. In the same process, He'll transform our sinful image into the likeness of Him.

It's impossible to avoid the process of sanctification; it's better to embrace it. Thankfully, God, the Holy Spirit, has promised to help in the process. He knows what you need to heal, and will lead you down the path of healing.

It's important to understand that the path of healing is narrow and difficult. God doesn't make it easy on you; He makes it possible. Healing requires humility. To heal, you must ask for help, admit your need, and leave your reputation in the hands of God. This is only possible when you allow God's grace to define you. If God didn't spare His Son so that you might be saved, He's not afraid to help you wash your socks. In fact, He's even given you brothers and sisters to wash them with you. In this way, sanctification happens by the power of God and with the help of others.

Although sanctification is a lifelong process, it doesn't excuse sin. You must participate in your sanctification. We'll discuss this in the next reading.

BIBLE PASSAGES

- **Romans 6:19** *csb* – '*I am using a human analogy because of the weakness of your flesh. For just as you offered the parts of yourselves as slaves to impurity, and to greater and greater lawlessness, so now offer them as slaves to righteousness, which results in sanctification.*'

- **1 Peter 1:14-16** *csb* – '*As obedient children, do not be conformed to the desires of your former ignorance. But as the one who called you is holy, you also are to be holy in all your conduct; for it is written, "Be holy, because I am holy."*'

- **1 Thessalonians 4:3-5** *csb* – '*For this is God's will, your sanctification: that you keep away from sexual immorality, that each of you knows how to control his own body in holiness and honor, not with lustful passions, like the Gentiles, who don't know God.*'

QUESTIONS FOR REFLECTION

1. Before reading this, did you believe that all of your baggage would disappear at the moment you trusted in Jesus? How does it make you feel knowing that it doesn't?

2. Do you understand how sanctification and justification are different? What does that tell you about the difference between salvation and Christian living?

3. The process of sanctification can be painful; are you committed to the process?

PRAYER

God, give me courage, wisdom, and help in the process of sanctification. Help me to be honest about areas in my life where I still 'smell like sin.' Help me to transform into the likeness of your son, Jesus.

*'The devil deals with men as the panther does with beasts; he
hides his deformed head until his sweet scent has drawn them
into his danger. Until we have sinned, Satan is a parasite; when we
have sinned, he is a tyrant.'* – Thomas Brooks[1]

Baggage Does Not Excuse Sin

In the first five years, my faith was rocky. I kept falling into serious sin. I got high, hung out with the wrong people, and regularly got into fights on the street and in the workplace. Of all my struggles, fighting was the hardest to overcome. I even pulled over on the freeway, with my family in the car, to fight someone who honked at me.

In my mind, it was always their fault. I wouldn't have had to fight if my boss had lowered his voice, if my coworker had had respect, and if the man in the grocery store had stopped staring at my wife. Over time, I recognized a pattern. The common thread in every situation was the pride in my heart. People will always sin against me, but it doesn't give me a license to sin against them. I could no longer blame my past for my current sinful behavior.

It's fashionable to make excuses for sin. You can point to your childhood, blame other people, or believe that you're a victim of circumstance. If things were different, you wouldn't act the way you do. However, God doesn't permit Christians to continue in sin; there's never a good reason. In fact, according to Scripture, those who

---

1. Thomas Brooks, *Precious Remedies Against Satan's Devices* (Feather Trail Press, 2010), 19.

remain in sin are not of Christ. This doesn't mean that Christians won't struggle with sin; it means that Christians don't make excuses for sin.

When you begin to follow Jesus, your past doesn't disappear. I still get pulled over by the police, and they even put me in handcuffs while they search my car. I used to get angry, but they don't know me. They don't know that I'm no longer a gangster. Some sin has consequences that will follow you to the grave. I may get pulled over for the rest of my life. Thankfully, they won't follow you into the grave. By the grace of God, we can escape some of the earthly consequences of sin; and by His power, we don't have to create more.

Following Jesus doesn't exempt you from pain. We live in a fallen world where people will sin against you, reject you, and even persecute you for your faith. When they do, we're commanded to love them in the same way that God has loved us. If I went around fighting everyone who sinned against me, I'd never see anyone come to Christ. I'd never learn the power of forgiveness, patience, or kindness.

As Christians, we can't make excuses for sin. We must acknowledge sin and repent of it. If we sin against others, we must confess our sin to them and ask for forgiveness. By making excuses, we don't give people the opportunity to heal. I've witnessed sin destroy relationships, take down gifted leaders, and ruin families. I've watched institutionalized sin poison society. Every person I know who isn't growing in their faith has unchecked sin in their life. Without confronting sin, we continue to hurt others. In sanctification, God will confront the sin in your life. There's no way to escape the process. If you don't deal with sin, it will deal with you.

Thankfully, you don't have to deal with sin alone. The Holy Spirit will help you defeat sin, the Church will walk with you in the process, and the Word of God will show you where you need to adjust. When you kill the sin in your life, it will stop killing you.

I sat in the parking lot of a new job and begged God to help me. I didn't want to fight anymore. I knew I was misrepresenting God and hurting myself. I called my friend from church and confessed my struggle to him. We prayed together, and I committed to repentance. I got out of the car and walked onto the job site. My new coworker was more difficult than any coworker I'd ever had. The Holy Spirit helped me to defeat the sin in my heart. I never got into a fight on that job, and my coworker met Jesus. The same coworker started the ministry that became the church I pastor today.

Confronting sin is a powerful weapon against Satan. As you see, God blesses repentance. He saved my coworker. For this reason, we must confront sin. In the next reading, we'll look at what it means to participate in your sanctification.

BIBLE PASSAGES

- **Romans 6:15-16** *CSB* – *'What then? Should we sin because we are not under the law but under grace? Absolutely not! Don't you know that if you offer yourselves to someone as obedient slaves, you are slaves of that one you obey – either of sin leading to death or of obedience leading to righteousness?'*

- **Romans 1:18-19** *CSB* – *'For God's wrath is revealed from heaven against all godlessness and unrighteousness of people who by their unrighteousness suppress the truth, since what can be known about God is evident among them, because God has shown it to them.'*

- **James 3:16** *CSB* – *'For where there is envy and selfish ambition, there is disorder and every evil practice.'*

QUESTIONS FOR REFLECTION

1. Do you make excuses for sin? Do you blame your past for sinful anger? Do you blame God for the need to turn towards worldly pleasures?

2. Is there something that you are currently unwilling to let go of? Which sin in your life provides a false sense of safety and comfort?

3. Do you believe that God wants to set you free and bring joy into your life? If so, why do you refuse to let it go? If not, what makes you believe that God doesn't want to increase your joy?

PRAYER

Jesus, you gave your life for the sins of the world. Help me never to excuse sin. Give me the power to overcome the sin in my life. By your Holy Spirit, show me where I need to turn from sin.

'We'll never make progress in holiness if we are waiting for the world to throw us a party for our piety... Becoming a living sacrifice, holy and acceptable to God, requires you to resist the world which wants to press you into its mold.' – Kevin De Young[1]

Dealing With Baggage Requires Your Participation

Earlier, we discussed the kids in my daughter's school. As they grow, they desperately want to figure out their identity. Many kids struggle to understand themselves and want to be accepted. To fit in, they rapidly change and try on sin like it's a new outfit. For example, they use new words and listen to new music. They don't want to be seen in public with their parents; and they treat their siblings poorly. They're very active in their transformation and in studying the people they admire.

We're used to kids acting this way, but adults do the same thing. We're just better at hiding it. We present our bodies to sin like it's a sport. We learn the language, buy the jersey, and show up to the court ready to play. We're professional sinners, and we've had a lot of practice. When the Bible talks about sanctification, it tells us to present ourselves to righteousness with the same energy. In fact, we must invest in sanctification with more energy than we invested in sin. We are called to be active in sanctification.

---

1. Kevin DeYoung, *The Hole in Our Holiness* (Wheaton: Crossway, 2012), 37, 38.

Remember, your actions don't earn your salvation. God doesn't accept us because we're gifted or because we work hard; He accepts us because of Jesus. For this reason, we don't participate in sanctification to earn God's love; we participate in sanctification because we know that God loves us. Christians participate in sanctification because we know that God is more satisfying than sin. In fact, if sin seems more satisfying than God, we should question whether or not we know Him.

The process of sanctification is a blessing from God. When you obey God, you experience His blessing, and your faith is strengthened. For this reason, those with the strongest faith will also have a history of obedience. When the safety inspector caught me breaking the rules, I could've lied or made an excuse. However, I knew the promise of God. Sin could not fix the sin I previously committed. I had to tell the truth and trust God with the outcome. That day, I got to keep my job, and my faith was strengthened.

In sanctification, the Bible says that we must put off the old self and put on the new man in Christ. Basically, we have to change our wardrobe. If we used to respond in anger, we need to respond with gentleness. If we're used to running from hard situations, we need to confront them with faith and with help from others. We have to dress for the occasion. We can't wear the same sinful habits and expect to grow. The reason we can participate in our sanctification is because we know that God accepts us in Christ. In this way, we don't have to hide or pretend we're perfect.

To put on the new self, we have to know who the new self is. The new self is made in the image of Jesus. For this reason, we need a lot of time with Jesus. We'll never respond like Jesus until we experience how He responds to us. He's gentle, patient, kind, and forgiving. He doesn't abandon us when it gets hard; instead, He sacrifices on our behalf.

We need to spend time learning about Jesus. For this, God gave us His Word. The Word of God reveals who Jesus is, how Jesus responds, and how Jesus is working in the world today. It reveals that the Church is the Body of Jesus. In this way, we learn that Jesus is known in His Church. For this reason, we need to actively participate in the Church so that we might know Jesus and make Him known.

Finally, God has given us His Holy Spirit. The Holy Spirit promises to bring to our mind the things of Jesus. He promises to help us obey Jesus, strengthen us when we're weak, and He promises to glorify Jesus in and through us. This means, to know Jesus, we must read His Word, participate in His Church, and spend a lot of time in prayer. Sanctification requires our participation.

Since sanctification is a process that occurs over the course of your life, it will happen in the everyday details. In the next reading, we'll discuss how sanctification happens in circumstance. However difficult the situation, you can be confident that God is working His process of sanctification in your life.

BIBLE PASSAGES

- **Ephesians 2:10** csb – 'For we are his workmanship, created in Christ Jesus for good works, which God prepared ahead of time for us to do.'

- **1 Corinthians 6:19-20** csb – 'Don't you know that your body is a temple of the Holy Spirit who is in you, whom you have from God? You are not your own, for you were bought at a price. So glorify God with your body.'

- **Titus 2:11-14** csb – 'For the grace of God has appeared, bringing salvation for all people, instructing us to deny godlessness and worldly lusts and to live in a sensible, righteous, and godly way in the present age, while we wait for the blessed hope, the appearing of the glory of our great God and Savior, Jesus Christ. He gave himself for us to redeem us from all lawlessness and to cleanse for himself a people for his own possession, eager to do good works.'

QUESTIONS FOR REFLECTION

1. What do you think it means to put off the old self and put on the new self in the likeness of Christ?

2. How have you given yourself over to sin in the past? What does it mean to be given over to godliness? How would you present yourself to godliness in the same way that you presented yourself to sin?

3. What should be your motivation for godliness? Who is the new self?

PRAYER

Lord, keep me active in my sanctification. Help me train for righteousness so that I may experience greater blessing in a relationship with you.

'The Holy Spirit often uses the emotional upheaval that accompanies disagreement and conflict to get our attention and drive us to make necessary changes in our families, churches, and personal lives.' – Alexander Strauch.[1]

The Process of Sanctification Happens in Circumstance

I met Jesus while incarcerated. In this particular institution, Christianity was viewed as a weakness. Many people would turn to God to avoid the hardship of incarceration but would return to their sin as soon as they were released. In this way, the chapel had a bad reputation. However, that wasn't my story. I indeed met Jesus and desired to follow Him. I was sincere. But, it didn't change the way people viewed my conversion. The next year would prove to be one of the hardest years of my life.

The institution was on permanent lockdown. An officer was murdered a few years before, and they decided to remove most of the programs. In response, inmates received an hour a day out of their cell. The rest of the time, we counted bricks to pass the day. Most people had cellmates to talk to, but my unit placed inmates in a single-man cell. At the time I met Jesus, I was locked in a cell for months with little relief.

---

1. Alexander Strauch, *If You Bite & Devour One Another* (Littleton: Lewis and Roth Publishers, 2011), 3.

What followed confused me. Other inmates mocked my decision and accused me of things that weren't true. They suspected I was another inmate trying to avoid the consequences of incarceration. People who knew me latched onto the crowd. This was a difficult time, and I was depressed. Somehow, the Holy Spirit gave me the strength to get through. Eventually, I was released, and so the story goes.

During this time, I thought I did something wrong. I doubted God and wondered if He failed me. However, looking back, the lesson is clear. God taught me endurance, the power of His Spirit, and the hostility you'll experience when you follow Jesus in the world. He also gave me a passion for training others. I wasn't prepared for my experience because no one prepared me. When I read the Bible, I learned that my experience was typical and should be expected. When you follow Jesus in a world that's opposed to Him, you can expect opposition. Finally, fifteen years later, many inmates have visited my church expressing an interest in Jesus. They remember those days and know that God is real.

This means sanctification isn't always about sin. God will allow hard circumstances into your life to strengthen your character and prepare you for the future. Other times, you'll experience pain because people are sinful. For this reason, you can trust God in whatever circumstance you may find yourself. God had a plan for my suffering beyond my understanding.

It's a great honor to suffer for God. By allowing suffering into your life, God invites you into His presence. God has experienced pain because of our sin, and He grieves the state of the world. This means suffering can be our most excellent teacher. By suffering, we gain a better understanding of God's love, since He suffered for us. In this way, we can trust God with our pain and trials. In every circumstance, God is working out His plan of sanctification in us.

As we respond to suffering in faith and obedience, we become an example to the world. In suffering, God purges us of any impurity and strengthens us. He sharpens our faith, and we become a weapon against the Liar. When Satan says that God has abandoned us, our stripes of victory tell another story. When I look back at the suffering in my life, I clearly see the goodness of God and the hopeless state of this world. God doesn't promise to protect you from pain, but He promises to be with you in it and to sanctify you by it.

Never doubt God. Though difficulties arise, God won't abandon you. By His Holy Spirit, He will sanctify you. In the next reading, we'll look at the role of the Holy Spirit in the process of sanctification.

BIBLE PASSAGES

- **2 Corinthians 12:7** csb – 'Therefore, so that I would not exalt myself, a thorn in the flesh was given to me, a messenger of Satan to torment me so that I would not exalt myself.'

- **Philippians 1:12-14** csb – 'Now I want you to know, brothers and sisters, that what has happened to me has actually advanced the gospel, so that it has become known throughout the whole imperial guard, and to everyone else, that my imprisonment is because I am in Christ. Most of the brothers have gained confidence in the Lord and dare even more to speak the word fearlessly.'

- **John 16:20** csb – 'Truly I tell you, you will weep and mourn, but the world will rejoice. You will become sorrowful, but your sorrow will turn to joy.'

QUESTIONS FOR REFLECTION

1. Are you confused by trials in your life? Do you trust God with your suffering?

2. Will you continue to trust God in obedience, even if He never gives you an answer as to why you experience trials?

3. What good have you seen come from previous trials? Since God can be trusted in all things, how should you respond when you don't understand?

PRAYER

God, help me to trust you in every circumstance. I know that you love me, and even subjected your son Jesus, to trials. Therefore, I can trust you in all things.

'If we interrupt the process of sanctification by procrastinating in meeting an issue that God has set before us or by reverting to a posture of backsliding unbelief, God in His love will inevitably bring our lives into circumstances of failure, frustration or suffering which will drive us back to sobriety.' – Richard Lovelace[1]

The Holy Spirit is Faithful to Sanctify You

As a father, there are many times my kids ask me to help them with difficult things. It may be homework, it could be a situation at school, or I might have to kill a spider. To be honest, it annoys me when I have to kill a spider. My kids are a thousand times bigger than a spider, and I don't understand why they freak out. However, they feel better when I'm around. They dare to accomplish difficult things just because I'm there. If they're in danger, they know I'll step in to protect them. If they struggle, they know I'll help. However, it doesn't mean that I'll make everything easy on them. Sometimes, I make them kill the spider on their own.

God hasn't called us to a process that we can't complete. Sanctification begins and ends with God. It starts at the moment we're saved and will end when God restores the world to Himself. We can expect to be in the process for our entire lives. For this reason, we don't get to be lazy. We must actively participate in our sanctification until the day we die. The good news is that God doesn't ask us to do this alone. Since He's

---

1. Richard Lovelace, *Dynamics of Spiritual Life* (Downers Grove: InterVarsity Press, 1979), 118.

in charge of the process, we can be sure that He'll also help us along the way. God is present in our sanctification. How's this possible? To understand God's presence, we have to look at what God says about Himself.

By this point, you may have realized that I've referred to God in three different ways. Jesus is God the Son, who died for sin, to restore the relationship between humans and God the Father. Jesus rose from the grave by the power of God the Holy Spirit, who also promises to empower Christians who trust in Jesus. So as you see, there is God the Father, God the Son, and God the Holy Spirit. God the Father is not God the Son and God the Son is not God the Holy Spirit. However, Jesus says, 'If you know Me, you will also know My Father. From now on you do know Him and have seen Him.' This is what Christians would call the Trinity. The Bible says that God is one, and reveals that God is three individual persons. How can this be so?

The Bible says that humans are created in the image of God. This means we reflect the nature of God. If you look at a shadow of a person on the ground, it reflects the person, but in no way does it show you how great the person actually is. In the same way, when God says that He is three persons, you can't look to the shadow (humans) to help you understand what He means by this. Often, we see three people, and we know that they're not one person, but three. So, when we hear that God is one, but read that He is three persons, we're confused. However, God's not like us; we're like Him. Therefore, our job is not to understand the Trinity but to accept it as true. This is important when we say that God is with us.

In the Bible, we read that God the Father is in heaven. We know that Jesus rose from the grave and He's there too. If God the Father is in Heaven, and God the Son is in Heaven, how is He with us? When we know that God is a Trinity, we see that God the Holy Spirit is always here. This means that God isn't too busy for you and is always available to help you when you're in need. Many believe that God doesn't want to help us, or that He's too far away. But, the reason Jesus rose from the grave was to send His Holy Spirit to us. In fact, His death made it possible. This should drive our thankfulness and love for Jesus. The same Holy Spirit who parted the Red Sea, who performed crazy miracles in Scripture, and raised Jesus from the grave is with believers.

The Holy Spirit is the one who sanctifies us. For this reason, we should never be afraid of anything. Instead, we should enter into every situation with confidence and faith. Our God is always with us.

In the next chapter, we'll look at the Church. One of the primary ways that God sanctifies believers is through the Church. The Church plays an essential role in the world and in the life of a Christian. For this reason, it's vital that our understanding of the Church is consistent with God's defined purpose for His Church, as revealed in the Bible.

BIBLE PASSAGES

- *John 14:26 csb* – 'But the Counselor, the Holy Spirit, whom the Father will send in my name, will teach you all things and remind you of everything I have told you.'

- *2 Thessalonians 2:13 csb* – 'But we ought to thank God always for you, brothers and sisters loved by the Lord, because from the beginning God has chosen you for salvation through sanctification by the Spirit and through belief in the truth.'

- *Romans 8:12-14 csb* – 'So then, brothers and sisters, we are not obligated to the flesh to live according to the flesh, because if you live according to the flesh, you are going to die. But if by the Spirit you put to death the deeds of the body, you will live. For all those led by God's Spirit are God's sons.'

QUESTIONS FOR REFLECTION

1. Do you understand why Jesus had to go to the Father? What benefit does that offer you?

2. How does the presence of God, the Holy Spirit, comfort you and lead you into doing what is right?

3. Do you feel like God is distant at times? What might God be teaching you in this feeling?

PRAYER

Holy Spirit, lead me into righteousness, sanctify me by your truth, and help me to see the beauty and majesty of Jesus.

Reflections

Summary

In a short paragraph, summarize what you've learned in this chapter:

....

....

....

....

....

....

....

....

Questions

Write down any questions you would like to ask at your next meet-up:

....

....

....

....

....

....

....

....

Summary

In a short paragraph, summarize what you've learned in this chapter.

Questions

Write down any questions you would like to ask at your next meet-up.

THE CHURCH

*'Jesus sacrificed Himself for others, and
Christians are called to do the same.'*

'A healthy church must model for a broken world a true fellowship or community of the Spirit; a "free space" where forgiveness is experienced and offered to all. A healthy church is a church of the toalla y palangana (towel and basin), serving the needy in and among them. A healthy church is ultimately by posture and program a worshipping congregation. It is a church that is constantly reminded that we worship one living God and not the many "idols" of our consumer society.' – Eldin Villafañe[1]

The Role of the Church in the World

Los Angeles is in my blood. I feel it every time I step off the plane after a trip away. I know I'm home as soon as I see the palm trees, concrete, and taco stands on the side of the road. There are distinct features about Los Angeles the natives feel in our bones. Often, I can identify an Angeleno anywhere in the country.

A few years ago, I found myself in Memphis, on Beale Street, in the rain. Looking across the street, I noticed a guy standing in front of a restaurant on the phone. Jokingly, I told my friend, 'I bet you that dude is from LA!' He thought I was crazy. I stepped up to the challenge and ran across the street. If we were gambling men, I would have had his money. I was correct. The man wasn't wearing any Los Angeles paraphernalia, and I'd never seen him before. I was

---

1. Eldin Villafañe, *Seek the Peace of the City* (Grand Rapids: Eerdmans, 1995), 10.

able to identify him by the way he carried himself. I knew that he was from Los Angeles.

Christians represent God in the world. The way a Christian carries himself should point to his citizenship in the Kingdom of God. This means, similar to how I knew that man was from Los Angeles, a Christian should be easily identifiable. Christians are identified by their love for others. They are known for their holy life and active commitment to Jesus. When I meet someone who loves his city, it always makes me want to visit. In the same way, when the world sees the Church, it should be attracted to Jesus. The Church is an army with a mission of proclaiming Christ in word and deed.

Through the Church, God is restoring the world to Himself as we speak. Every Christian has been deployed to the task and is placed on active duty. This means the Church isn't a private club that judges the world from afar. Instead, it engages the world and sacrifices on its behalf. Jesus sacrificed Himself for others, and Christians are called to do the same. Christians stand for what is right, fight against what is wrong, and proclaim Jesus in all of life. When each Christian is living out his God-given design, the Church is effective.

As Christians work together toward God's will, the Church is a global family on mission. There are different denominations, and each church is unique. But, every Christian church agrees on the essential things. All Christians believe that Jesus is God and in His virgin birth. They believe in the resurrection, and that salvation is in Jesus alone. Christians believe in the Trinity and that the Bible is true. They believe that Jesus will return to judge the living and the dead. If you deny any of these beliefs, you're not a Christian. All Christian churches affirm these truths. In this way, God is working in all parts of the world, in different ways, through His one global Church. The Church is a global family that's reaching the world.

As you can see, the Church is not a place or a building. It's also not a self-help organization. The Church is a people united together in pursuit of God. The Church is joined together to fulfill God's mission in the world. For this reason, every Christian must join a local church. There's no such thing as a healthy Christian who's not committed to the Church. I recognize that finding a local church can be difficult. No church is perfect, and every church will have problems. But, the Church is effective. When choosing a local church, you should be asking, 'Is it biblical, and is God deploying me to this post?'

At the end of this chapter, we'll look at how to identify a healthy church. But first, it's important to understand the relationship every Christian should have with the Church.

BIBLE PASSAGES

- **Colossians 4:2-6** *csb* – *'Devote yourself to prayer; stay alert in it with thanksgiving. At the same time pray also for us that God may open a door to us for the word, to speak the mystery of Christ, for which I am in chains, so that I may make it known as I should. Act wisely towards outsiders, making the most of the time. Let your speech always be gracious, seasoned with salt, so that you may know how you should answer each person.'*

- **Ephesians 1:9-10** *csb* – *'He made known to us the mystery of his will, according to his good pleasure that he purposed in Christ as a plan for the right time – to bring everything together in Christ, both things in heaven and things on earth in him.'*

- **Matthew 28:18-20** *csb* – *'Jesus came near and said to them, "All authority has been given to me in heaven and on earth. Go, therefore, and make disciples of all nations, baptizing them in the name of the Father and of the Son and of the Holy Spirit, teaching them to observe everything I have commanded you. And remember, I am with you always, to the end of the age."'*

QUESTIONS FOR REFLECTION

1. Before reading this, did you view the Church as an organization that exists to meet your needs or as a people that God is using to change the world?

2. Are you currently invested in a local church? If so, it should show in how you spend your time, how you use your talents, and how you use the resources God has given you (money; possessions; skills).

3. Are you committed to living in such a way that others might be interested in Jesus because of your example? Do you see yourself as a representative of Jesus in the world? Would others agree?

PRAYER

God, help me to live for you and not for me since you know what's best for me and since you can use me to be a blessing to others.

'Come, meet my big, crazy, messed up, extended family,' we say. 'There you will find the love, care, and burden-bearing relationships for which you crave.' – Dustin Willis.[1]

The Role of the Church in the Christian

When I worked in construction, the conversations during lunch saddened me. Everyone always complained about their wives – it was confusing. I wondered why anyone would marry a person they despised. I also wondered why a person would want others to see their wife so negatively? Marriage is a beautiful gift from God. My wife is my best friend, and I want to spend the rest of my life with her. I won't tolerate anyone speaking poorly of my wife. She's not perfect, but she's my wife – and I love her.

The Bible refers to the Church as the Bride of Christ. In this way, Jesus is the groom, and He's not like the men sitting around lunchboxes at the job site. Jesus doesn't complain about His bride. Instead, He protects her and provides for her needs. If you're a Christian, Jesus promises to care for you. It's important to understand the way that Jesus cares for His bride to experience all that He has for you. The primary way that Jesus will care for you is through the local church.

The local church is made up of different people with diverse gifts. For this reason, the Bible also refers to the Church as the Body

---

1. Dustin Willis, *Life in Community* (Chicago: Moody Publishers, 2015), 16.

of Christ. God has uniquely created each individual to fit with other Christians. When one part of the Body is sick or wounded, it affects the entire body. But when the body is healthy, it's effective. In the same way, when Christians work together, we're effective. Led by the Holy Spirit, Christians love one another, meet needs, and carry heavy burdens. In the Book of Acts, we read about believers selling their possessions and distributing them to those in need. God will meet your needs in the local church.

Don't be confused – the Bride of Christ and the local church are not separate. Each member of the Body of Christ makes up the Bride of Christ. In this way, the Body of Christ and the Bride of Christ are metaphors that help us to understand our identity as Christians.

The local church is also the school of sanctification, and that is one of the primary ways God meets our needs. As we have seen, we have a deep need to be sanctified. The local church is where we learn to obey God under the authority of appointed leaders who teach and enforce the Scriptures. It's where we partake of communion, which is a profession of our need for Christ. In the local church, we are held accountable and are challenged to grow. We're corrected when we sin, encouraged when we're struggling, and helped when we're weak. There's no such thing as a healthy Christian who's not committed to a local church!

Early on, I struggled as a Christian. I recall a time where I was disconnected from the local church. My marriage was struggling, and my wife gave birth to our second daughter. I decided to barbecue and invited a group of friends. We lived in a dangerous area, and my friends were gangsters. During the barbecue, there was a knock at the door. It was a pastor and a group of Christians. They had heard that I was struggling and had come to encourage me. We had guns, drugs, and were up to no good. But, this group of Christians didn't care. They showed up to love me. They came every night for the next two weeks and encouraged me to join a group. This changed my life. Jesus cared for me through His Church.

Everyone has needs. Your life may not be as messed up as mine, but you have blind spots. When they surface, God intends to care for you through His Church. God will also use you to care for others. You may be the one to knock on the door of a gangster like me. In doing so, God will teach you about His love and mercy.

There are no such things as Christian nomads. God does not intend for believers to be disconnected from one another. Jesus cares for His bride by placing Christians in an environment where they will thrive. He puts them in the context of the local church. As you can see, the Church plays a role in the world by playing a role in the Christian. When Christians experience the love of Jesus, often through His Church, they are compelled to share this love with others.

BIBLE PASSAGES

- **Acts 2:44-47** *csb* – *'Now all the believers were together and held all things in common. They sold their possessions and property and distributed the proceeds to all, as any had need. Every day they devoted themselves to meeting together in the temple, and broke bread from house to house. They ate their food with joyful and sincere hearts, praising God and enjoying the favor of all the people. Every day the Lord added to their number those who were being saved.'*

- **Ephesians 4:15-16** *csb* – *'But speaking the truth in love, let us grow in every way into him who is the head – Christ. From him the whole body, fitted and knit together by every supporting ligament, promotes the growth of the body for building up itself in love by the proper working of each individual part.'*

- **John 13:34-35** *csb* – *'I give you a new command: Love one another. Just as I have loved you, you are also to love one another. By this everyone will know that you are my disciples, if you love one another.'*

QUESTIONS FOR REFLECTION

1. In the local church, do you have meaningful relationships where you can be honest, open, and share your real struggles?

2. Are you available to meet the needs of others? Or, do you only make your own needs known?

3. Will you commit to being someone others can count on?

PRAYER

God, help the Church be all that it can be in the world. Please bless my local church. Help me to experience the benefits of a healthy church so that I may be a blessing to others.

'The isolated Christian can indeed know something of the love of Jesus. But his grasp of it is bound to be limited by his limited experience. It needs the whole people of God to understand the whole love of God, all the saints together, Jews and Gentiles, men and women, young and old, black and white, with all their varied backgrounds and experiences.' – John Stott[1]

The Role of the Christian in the Church

We need to stop lying. Every third grader in America can't be president. In fact, it's statistically impossible. If everyone ran for president at the same time, only one person would be chosen. In the same way, not every singer will be famous. Some singers can't even sing. Countless people who want to be rich and famous move to Los Angeles every day. Many of them should go home. The truth is, you can't be anything you want to be. The good news is that you don't have to be.

Many of the desires we have don't originate with us. Some people want to please their parents. So, they go to college to pursue a career that will make their father happy. Other people have something to prove; they may have been bullied as a child. In response, they pursue power and independence in the workforce. Finally, some people look at what others have and assume they'd

---

1. John Stott, *The Message to Ephesians* (Downers Grove: InterVarsity Press, 1979), 137.

be happy if they had the same. Many people struggle with anxiety, depression, and loneliness because they're trying to fill shoes that aren't theirs to fill.

Humans weren't created with the ability to be whatever they desire. God created you with a specific role to play in the world. He gave you the gifts, talents, and opportunities you have for a reason: you're to serve God with them. Your deepest satisfaction will come when you live according to the purpose God has for your life. Many people have a hard time discovering this purpose. Thankfully, God didn't make it complicated.

For one, God gave us the Bible. In the Bible, He makes it clear that humans were created for Him. In this way, we're to live our lives to please God. When you seek God in prayer, He'll reveal His purpose in His Word.

Next, we know that the world is broken and God is in the process of restoring it. This means we're to participate in repairing the world. If what we desire contradicts the Bible, we shouldn't crave it; if it doesn't bring about restoration in the world, we shouldn't be a part of it. In prayer, God will show us *how* He's restoring the world, and *how* we can join Him.

Finally, God has given us gifts, talents, and opportunities. If we have the capability, and the support of God's Word, we should do what we desire; if we don't, we shouldn't. Since God has placed others in our lives to help us grow, other people who love God will support the things that God desires. God will lead them by His Holy Spirit. If trusted friends don't support your decisions, you should proceed with caution or abandon the idea altogether. So you see, it's relatively simple to discover the will of God for your life.

If you have a role to play in the world, you also have a role to play in the Church. Remember the orchestra? When every instrument works together, a beautiful sound is made. In the same way, when every member of the church functions according to God's purpose, the Church is a beautiful sound in the world. When members of the church refuse to participate, or desire to operate in a way that God never intended, it's bad for everyone. This means the Church can't be all that it's designed to be without you.

The Church is not a place where professionals put on a show. As we've already identified, the Church is a family and an army; every member matters. God will use you to lead someone to Jesus, to speak into another person's life, and to ensure that His mission goes forward. He'll do so through your time, talents, and even your treasures. In the same way, He'll provide for your deepest needs through the time, talents, and treasures of others.

So you see, the Church plays a crucial role in the world as each Christian plays their role in the Church. I wish it wasn't complicated, but it is. For this reason, I've devoted the next reading to discussing the reality of the Church.

BIBLE PASSAGES

- *1 Corinthians 12:4-7 csb* – *'Now there are different gifts, but the same Spirit. There are different ministries, but the same Lord. And there are different activities, but the same God produces each gift in each person. A manifestation of the Spirit is given to each person for the common good.'*

- *1 Corinthians 12:12 csb* – *'For just as the body is one and has many parts, and all the parts of that body, though many, are one body–so also is Christ.'*

- *1 Corinthians 12:20-22 csb* – *'As it is, there are many parts, but one body. The eye cannot say to the hand, "I don't need you!" Or again, the head can't say to the feet, "I don't need you!" On the contrary, those parts of the body that are weaker are indispensable.'*

QUESTIONS FOR REFLECTION

1. Do you know that you are extremely valuable and are very much needed in the local church?

2. The Bible teaches that God has intentionally placed you in the world at this point in history—and has equipped you—to advance His cause in the world. Do you believe this?

3. Have you refused to participate in the local church? Why? Will you choose to participate from this point forward?

PRAYER
God, thank you for loving me and valuing me. Thank you for giving me a purpose in this world and using me to advance your mission. Help me to serve others and be faithful with all that you have entrusted to me.

'Every human wish/dream [fantasy] that is injected into the [reality of the] Christian community is a hindrance to genuine community and must be banished if genuine community is to survive. He who loves his dream of a community more than the Christian community itself becomes a destroyer of the latter, even though his personal intentions may be ever so honest and earnest and sacrificial.' – Dietrich Bonhoeffer[1]

The Reality of the Local Church

Sometimes, romantic movies annoy me. They're hardly ever true. Real life doesn't have a soundtrack; and every couple fights. When I meet people who say they don't, they haven't been married long enough, have zero intimacy with their spouse, or they're destined for divorce. I don't mean to be negative, but it's true. There has never been a time in history where sinners who have committed to one another don't sin against each other. Movies present love in a way that's just false.

I've been married for many years, and my wife and I have had our share of arguments. At times, we've had to ask for help from others. Other times, we've had to accept the fact that we just don't agree. Our marriage isn't strong because everything is perfect; our marriage is secure because of our commitment to one another and our commitment to God. I don't need my wife to be perfect, and I don't need her to be just like me. In fact, over time, I've learned that my wife is different because God created her that way. Our differences make us better. I trust

---

1. Dietrich Bonhoeffer, *Life Together* (New York: HarperCollins Publishers, 1954), 27.

my wife because we have a history of commitment. I know that she won't leave when things get difficult, and I know that she has my best interests in mind. I'm committed to my marriage, but it's not always easy.

The reality of the Church is similar to that of marriage. God calls Christians to commit to one another. This means, like marriage, it's not always easy. When Christians commit to one another over an extended period of time, they'll argue, sin against each other, and need the help of others. At times, they'll have to agree to disagree. God will use the local church to make you better. However, your growth will depend upon your commitment to the church and your devotion to God and each other. If you run every time it gets difficult, you'll never experience the fullness of what God has in store for you through His Church.

Many professing Christians view the local church as a romantic movie. For some reason, they assume the church is a place where professionals put on a show. They're surprised when it's complicated, and they're confused when there's conflict. When the church doesn't have a program they desire, they move on. However, we're not always good at knowing what we need. God calls us to participate in His mission, not just receive from it. Maybe you're the one who needs to start the program. Or, maybe your expectations are too high.

One expectation Christians should have (but rarely do) is that there will be conflict. But conflict is not always bad. Sometimes, conflict is necessary for growth. In fact, conflict is a regular occurrence in the Bible. Remember, sanctification happens within circumstances. Learning how to resolve conflict is part of growing in maturity. You don't have to forgive someone who doesn't offend you, you don't have to be patient with someone who never gets on your nerves, and you don't have to carry anyone's burdens when everything is taken care of. You see, God will grow you the most in relationships with difficult people, through difficult circumstances, over an extended period of time. As a result, you'll learn to love others as God loves you. Real church is hard, but it's also great. For this reason, it's essential that every Christian commits to a local church and participates.

Now, there are churches that you should avoid. You should avoid a church where Jesus isn't at the center. This means the preaching and focus of the church should always center on who Jesus is, what

He has done, and what that means. Healthy churches believe the Bible is true and obey what it teaches. They also care for the lost, hold each other accountable, and teach others to obey Jesus. In a healthy church, there isn't one person in charge. Instead, the church is led by a group of men who practice what they preach. In a healthy church, people meet Jesus and grow in their relationship with Him. In the next reading, we'll discuss how to identify a healthy church.

BIBLE PASSAGES

- *1 Peter 1:6-7* csb – *'You rejoice in this, even though now for a short time, if necessary you suffer grief in various trials so that the proven character of your faith—more valuable than gold which, though perishable, is refined by fire—may result in praise, glory, and honor at the revelation of Jesus Christ.'*

- *James 4:11-12* csb – *'Don't criticize one another, brothers and sisters. Anyone who defames or judges a fellow believer defames and judges the law. If you judge the law, you are not a doer of the law but a judge. There is one lawgiver and judge who is able to save and to destroy. But who are you to judge your neighbor?'*

- *1 Corinthians 1:11* csb – *'For it has been reported to me about you, my brothers and sisters, by members of Chloe's people, that there is rivalry among you.'*

QUESTIONS FOR REFLECTION

1. Do you have a fantasy view of the Church? If so, do you place expectations on the Church that are unfair?

2. Do you avoid conflict? Do believe that all conflict is bad? How can conflict be good? Since the Bible teaches us how to resolve conflict in the Church, should we be surprised when it comes up?

3. What is the benefit of remaining in a difficult scenario over an extended period of time?

PRAYER

Lord, help me have realistic expectations for other people. Help me not to judge your Bride wrongly. Give me the strength to love others in the same way that Jesus has loved me.

'A healthy church is not a church that's perfect and without sin. It has not figured everything out. Rather, it's a church that continually strives to take God's side in the battle against the ungodly desires and deceits of the world, our flesh, and the devil. It's a church that continually seeks to conform itself to God's Word.' – Mark Dever[1]

Identifying a Healthy Local Church

This summer, I get to perform the marriage ceremony for a couple in our church. I do this regularly; however, this one is special. The groom and I were from the same gang. Now, we serve the same God. Recently, we had the opportunity to share the Gospel at a funeral of a fellow gang member. Following the funeral, we joined forces, and he joined the church. Soon after, he began to date a woman in the congregation, and they're getting married. The only thing is, they want to get married in Belize.

Traveling to Belize is different than traveling throughout the States. Usually, I'm confident in new environments, and I don't have a problem in rough areas. As I prepare for my trip, I'm having a difficult time knowing how to get around, where to eat, and how much money to bring. I don't understand the laws, and I don't want the locals to take advantage of us. I'm excited about the trip, but the research is overwhelming.

---

1. Mark Dever, *What is a Healthy Church* (Wheaton: Crossway, 2007), 40.

Finding a healthy church can be overwhelming; it can feel like my trip to Belize. In a foreign country, eating at a bad restaurant or turning down the wrong street can make you sick or put you in danger. A lousy church can do the same. On the other hand, there are beautiful streets you should turn down with beautiful places where you'll make fascinating discoveries. Similarly, there are healthy churches you should commit to joining. To do so, you need to know what a healthy church looks like. Since the local church is far more important than a vacation, you need biblical guidelines, and you need to do the research.

Good churches come in all shapes and sizes. There are benefits and disadvantages to small and big churches alike. Some churches have a great music team and terrible preaching. Other churches have great teaching but don't have ways for members to get involved. Finally, some churches are very active but aren't healthy at all. What should you look for in a local church? Since healthy churches have different structures, I want to identify three things that will mark every healthy church.

The Gospel

The Gospel is literally the *good news* of Jesus. We learned that humans are sinful and deserve punishment for sin. We also learned that God sent Jesus to rescue sinful humanity by offering His life as a payment for sin. In doing so, everyone who calls upon the name of Jesus and turns away from sin is forgiven because of His sacrifice. We know that those who trust in Jesus are also righteous because of Him. Although every church is different, a healthy church will have a culture that is marked by the Gospel.

For example, a healthy church will preach the Gospel, demonstrate the Gospel, and share the Gospel with others. In everything, you should be able to identify how Jesus is the hero. Members should care for the lost, and live holy lives; and the church should be marked by grace and generosity.

The Bible

A healthy church will submit to the Scriptures. Clarifying this point is essential. Submitting to the Scriptures doesn't mean reading them or quoting them only. Often, what is called Scriptural is actually one man's opinion of the Scriptures. Healthy churches will submit to the Scriptures by looking for the original interpretation of the text and showing how it fits into the whole Bible.

In this way, a healthy church will have biblical leadership, biblical church membership, and will call its members to obey the Bible in its entirety. When you look at the structure and message of a healthy church, Scripture will always support it.

Biblical Leadership

Finally, healthy churches are led by a group of men called elders. Elders care for the church, protect it, and equip the church to fulfill her mission in the world. Elders meet the qualifications laid out in the Bible, and there's always more than one. This protects the church from the abuse of power and ensures that every pastor is held accountable.

Finding a healthy church is not impossible. Some churches will be healthier than others, but no church is perfect. It's vital that you identify a healthy church and get involved. Your level of involvement actually contributes to the health of a church for good or for bad.

Now that you know what God is doing in your life and in the world, it's important to understand what it means to walk with God. In the next chapter, we'll discuss the basics of walking with God. And in doing so, I hope that you not only learn about walking with God, but instead, *choose* to walk with Him. In that final day, when God judges the world, there will be many people who will be confused. They'll have spent their entire life doing religious things, without actually walking with God. The Bible tells us that God will reject those people, only because He never knew them.

BIBLE PASSAGES

- **Romans 1:16** *CSB* – 'For I am not ashamed of the gospel, because it is the power of God for salvation to everyone who believes, first to the Jew, and also to the Greek.'

- **2 Timothy 4:2** *CSB* – 'Preach the word; be ready in season and out of season; rebuke, correct, and encourage with great patience and teaching.'

- **Hebrews 13:17** *CSB* – *'Obey your leaders and submit to them, since they keep watch over your souls as those who will give an account, so that they can do this with joy and not with grief, for that would be unprofitable for you.'*

QUESTIONS FOR REFLECTION

1. Do you feel capable of identifying a healthy church? Is your church healthy?

2. Do you read the Bible regularly? If you don't read the Bible, will you be able to recognize when a church is unhealthy?

3. God has structured the local church under the leadership of local pastor/elders. Do you have problems with authority? Why is authority good?

PRAYER

God, I pray for healthy churches. I pray for the leaders in my own church, that you would protect them from dishonoring you. Help me to follow my leaders as they follow Christ.

Reflections

Summary

In a short paragraph, summarize what you've learned in this chapter:

....
....
....
....
....
....
....
....

Questions

Write down any questions you would like to ask at your next meet-up:

....
....
....
....
....
....
....
....

WEEK 6

WALKING WITH GOD

'God will use every circumstance to draw you into a space where you experience him.'

*'The experiences of men who walked with God in
olden times agree to teach that the Lord cannot
fully bless a man until He has first conquered him.
The degree of blessing enjoyed by any man will
correspond exactly with the completeness of God's
victory over him.'* – A. W. Tozer[1]

A People That Walk With God

Over the past few years, I've tremendously benefited from a group of older men. I feel honored to have them in my life. Surrounding yourself with mentors is essential. To do so, you must remain humble and be willing to listen. Many people lack mentors because they're unwilling to take advice. These people almost always learn the hard way.

Yesterday, I became frustrated with a situation that occurred between two of my friends. I wanted to resolve the situation immediately. Unfortunately, that wasn't going to happen. As a result, I reached out to one of my mentors for counsel. He explained that he'd learned a crucial lesson in his fifty years of ministry. In this time, he came to realize that things weren't as urgent as they first appeared to be. He reminded me that God is always in control and will move as quickly or slowly as He desires.

As we consider all that we've learned, it's important to note that Christian growth happens over a lifetime. I'm ambitious, and I like things to move fast. When trials come, I'm quick to question

---

1. A. W. Tozer, *God's Pursuit of Man* (Chicago: Moody Publishers, 1950).

God. Thankfully, He isn't shaken by my temper tantrums or by my complaining. I'm not the best manager of my life, and my plans are shortsighted. God knows what I need, and ultimately, that I need Him. It may happen quickly, or it may occur over many years – but in all things, God is always drawing me into a space where I experience Him.

The Christian life is about walking with God. In the Bible, the story of Moses is a prime example of this. Moses was an Israelite who was born into captivity. At the time of his birth, the king of Egypt commanded the midwives to kill every male child who was born to the Israelites. The Israelites were growing in number, and the king was afraid of them. To save her son, Moses' mother placed him in a basket and sent him down the river. The king's daughter found Moses and raised him as her own.

Years later, Moses learned that the Egyptians mistreated the Israelites. They were abused and were forced into labor. On one occasion, he witnessed an Egyptian beat an Israelite man. Moses stood up for the man and killed the Egyptian. When the king found out, he wanted Moses dead. In response, Moses fled from Egypt to escape punishment. The Egyptians continued to oppress the Israelites.

Many years later, God spoke to Moses in an unusual way. While he was working in the field, he came across a strange bush. As he approached the bush, he realized it was burning. Interestingly, it was not consumed. Then, the voice of God spoke to him from the bush. God told Moses to return to Egypt and confront the king. God told Moses that He would use him to deliver the Israelites out of captivity. Moses obeyed. He returned to Egypt.

After the king resisted, the people were released. The circumstances and events that took place after the release are enough to drive any man crazy. God performed many miracles to deliver His people. Eventually, he defeated the king of Egypt by miraculous power. The Israelites saw these miracles one by one. Still, after their release, when things became difficult, the people complained, doubted God, and blamed Moses.

Moses began his life as an orphan. Eventually, his own grandfather wanted him dead. Throughout his life, he struggled with insecurity.

His own people blamed him for their suffering and regularly made his life difficult. Even though God would use Moses more than any other prophet, He required him to live by faith the entire time. Moses had to obey a bush, confront a superpower, and rely on God to perform miracles every step of the way. At the end of his life, we learn in the Scriptures, 'No prophet has risen again in Israel like Moses, whom the LORD knew face to face' (Deut. 34:10 CSB).

As we see with Moses, walking with God is difficult. However, we see that God knows what we need. He asked an insecure man to live by faith so that He could heal him. God took an orphan and drew him to His face. The same God who came to Moses is the same God who comes to us. God will use every circumstance to pull you into a space where you experience Him. Your job is to walk with Him, wherever He leads you, for the rest of your life.

How do we know how to walk with God? Many people say they walk with God, but instead follow a god of their own making. For this reason, God has given us the Bible. In the Bible, God shows us how to walk with Him. Christians are a people of the Book. In the next reading, we'll discuss what it means to follow God, as He has revealed Himself in His Word.

BIBLE PASSAGES

- **James 4:8** *CSB* – *'Draw near to God, and he will draw near to you. Cleanse your hands, sinners, and purify your hearts, you double-minded.'*

- **John 15:5** *CSB* – *'I am the vine; you are the branches. The one who remains in me and I in him produces much fruit, because you can do nothing without me.'*

- **Deuteronomy 34:10** *CSB* – *'No prophet has risen again in Israel like Moses, whom the LORD knew face to face.'*

QUESTIONS FOR REFLECTION

1. Do you want rapid growth, or are you prepared to walk with God over a lifetime?

2. Do you want to know God, or do you want things from God?

3. Do you trust God with the extent of your life? Do you believe that He loves you and that he wants what's best for you?

PRAYER

God, help me to desire you. Lead me into a personal and intimate relationship with you. Help me identify the areas in my life where I'm afraid to trust you.

'Since "all Scripture is breathed out by God and profitable for teaching, for reproof, for correction, and for training in righteousness" (2 Tim. 3:16 ESV), shouldn't we read it?' – Donald Whitney[1]

A People of the Book

Last month, I was diagnosed with an illness. Apparently, the doctors say there's no cure. I believe that God can heal me, but if He chooses not to, I want to learn how to take care of my body. As I began to research the illness, I quickly became overwhelmed. The research contradicts itself, and the doctors don't agree on the cause of the disease or the treatment for it.

Each person has a different conclusion, and I don't know which one to believe. The same can be said for a lot of things. With access to the Internet, the amount of information at our fingertips will leave the average man paralyzed. There's a study proving everything. Unfortunately, if everything is correct, nothing is to be trusted.

It makes sense why God gave us the Bible. As information increases, we have an anchor that doesn't move. We don't have to rely on new information, and we don't have to anxiously await future discoveries. Everything we need to know about God, about humanity, and about the future has been revealed. God has shown it to us in the Bible.

---

1. Donald S. Whitney, *Spiritual Disciplines for the Christian Life* (Colorado Springs: NavPress, 1991, 2014), 27.

Christians are people of the Book. We believe that the Bible contains the words of God. For this reason, Christians read the Bible, study it, and obey what it teaches. In fact, the Bible itself tells us to do so. If you don't believe the Bible, you're not a Christian. Therefore, it's essential that everything you believe about God is consistent with whom He has revealed Himself to be in the Bible.

Many people aren't informed about the truthfulness of the Bible. Often, when people make claims against the Bible, they haven't actually researched the subject for themselves. Usually, they repeat things they've heard from other people without checking to see if what they're saying is actually true. However, when you look at the evidence, the Bible doesn't need any protection. It can withstand the fiercest critique. For this reason, I'm not going to argue for the authenticity of the Bible. Others have done a far better job than I can do. Instead, I want to encourage you to read your Bible and obey what it says.

The Bible is a collection of writings written by forty different authors, over a span of 1500 years, on three different continents. Within these writings, some books detail the history of the world, tell of the future, share the personal experiences of various people, detail eyewitness accounts of Jesus, and contain letters to early churches written by Christian leaders. It's likely none of the authors knew that their words would eventually form the Bible. However, everything that's written tells a complete story. It's marvelous.

When reading the Bible, it's important to work towards understanding that complete story. In doing so, you'll learn who God is, what He's done, what He's currently doing, and what He's going to do in the future. Everything you learn will prepare you to serve Him now.

Christians must make a regular practice of reading the Bible. Many professing Christians don't read the Bible and remain immature. They're easily overtaken by the schemes of the Enemy. They have no way to defend themselves against the lies of Satan because they have no idea what's true.

It's only upon reading the Bible, and obeying what it says, that you'll see its truth come to life. Those who obey the Bible experience its blessings and avoid the consequences of disobedience. Those who know the Bible know their God.

Don't be afraid of the Bible. Ask others for help when you don't understand. When reading the Bible, make sure you pray beforehand, know who the author is, seek to understand what's happening in the story, and read entire books in order. Don't just open up your Bible to any page. People believe wrong things about God because they read a text without considering how it fits into the larger story. Read the Bible from the beginning to the end and don't get discouraged if it takes you a few years. You can get through it with God's help and the support of His people.

Scripture was written by the inspiration of God's Holy Spirit. In the next reading, we'll learn how the Holy Spirit of God empowers each Christian individually.

BIBLE PASSAGES

- **2 Timothy 3:16-17** *CSB* – *'All Scripture is inspired by God and is profitable for teaching, for rebuking, for correcting, for training in righteousness, so that the man of God may be complete, equipped for every good work.'*

- **Psalm 119:9** *CSB* – *'How can a young man keep his way pure? By keeping your word.'*

- **Matthew 7:24-27** *CSB* – *'Therefore, everyone who hears these words of mine and acts on them will be like a wise man who built his house on the rock. The rain fell, the rivers rose, and the winds blew and pounded that house. Yet it didn't collapse, because its foundation was on the rock. But everyone who hears these words of mine and doesn't act on them will be like a foolish man who built his house on the sand. The rain fell, the rivers rose, the winds blew and pounded that house, and it collapsed. It collapsed with a great crash.'*

QUESTIONS FOR REFLECTION

1. Have you read the entire Bible? If not, will you commit to doing so? If you have, are you committed to obeying what you learned?

2. Since God has shared all that we need to know about Him in the Bible, can a Christian have a healthy relationship with God

apart from studying His Word? What dangers are associated with believing only some parts of the Bible?

3. What benefits do you think there are in learning the history of the Bible?

PRAYER

God, thank you for speaking to us through the Bible. Help me to understand and obey what I read and to have the discipline to study your words daily.

'Trying to do the Lord's work in your own strength is the most confusing, exhausting, and tedious of all work. But when you are filled with the Holy Spirit, then the ministry of Jesus just flows out of you.' – Corrie Ten Boom[1]

A People of the Spirit

Every so often, I dream about having a superpower. If I could have just one, it would be the power to become invisible. When I consider why this power is attractive, it's attached to my pain. I don't trust people, and I have a hard time trusting God. Close friends have betrayed me, and my earthly father always broke his promises. If I could become invisible, I'd have the ability to find out the truth about people and situations. I'd have the ability to protect myself from pain. At least, that's what I'd be tempted to believe. However, I don't have a superpower, and I'll never have one in this life. I can't protect myself from pain, and I can't control the outcome of situations. But, I'm not powerless.

Thankfully, God isn't like my earthly father. He doesn't break His promises; and He's able to protect me. He's even given me the power to be successful in the world in the things He's called me to do. God has empowered me to fulfill His plan for my life and to live boldly for Him. I don't have to worry about protecting myself. In fact, I don't have to live for myself at all. Since God loves me, and I belong to Him, it's His responsibility to meet my needs. For this reason, I get to live

---

1. Corrie Ten Boom, *Tramp for the Lord* (Fort Washington: CLC Publication, 2010), 63.

my life thinking about pleasing God and serving others. This brings true freedom and satisfaction. Every true follower of Christ should think this way.

God empowers Christians through His Holy Spirit. When Jesus rose from the grave, He went up to the Father in heaven so that He could send His Holy Spirit. Before He died and resurrected, humans had no direct access to God. Like a wall, sin separated sinful humans from God. However, God accepted the sacrifice of Jesus and promised to forgive everyone who comes to the Father through Him. This means everyone who repents of his sin and trusts in Jesus for salvation has access to God.

God hasn't just given us access in the form of communication. Instead, He sent His own Spirit to live inside true believers. In this way, every Christian has access to the power of God's Holy Spirit – the same Spirit who parted the sea and raised Jesus from the grave. No superpower can match the power that true believers possess.

Imagine that! If you're a Christian, the Holy Spirit of God empowers you. More significant than any superhero team, the Holy Spirit has distributed specific spiritual gifts to each Christian. In this way, each member of Christ's Church is specially empowered to serve God. This means you have been given specific, and sometimes multiple spiritual gifts to empower you. For this reason, Christians are not powerless. God has empowered them with His Holy Spirit.

The Bible teaches that the gifts of the Spirit are for the building up of the Body of Christ. When each gift works together, the Church is a force not to be reckoned with.

If Christians find their power in the Holy Spirit, then they're powerless apart from Him. Since the Holy Spirit gives us victory, it's impossible to accomplish the mission of God apart from our spiritual gifts. Since it's the Spirit of God who saves believers, we must spend time listening to the Holy Spirit, and follow His lead. God will guide us to specific people and use our particular gifts to draw them to salvation. God will strengthen us by the gifts of others and will use our gifts to strengthen them.

As you can see, it's a great privilege to have access to the Holy Spirit of God. If you neglect a relationship with the Holy Spirit, you overlook the most significant power that you have as a Christian, and the intimate access you have to God. For this reason, there's much confusion with regard to the Holy Spirit.

Some people are obsessed with miraculous experiences, and—in so doing—misrepresent the Spirit. They expect the Holy Spirit to show up with signs and wonders all of the time. However, once we observe the character of God, we see that God is strategic in all of His miracles. When God displays His miraculous power, He does so for a particular purpose. For this reason, we can't assume that God will show up in miraculous power just because we ask Him to. Instead, we can be sure that God will do what's best for us—and for others—all of the time. We can trust God, even if He leads us down a scary path where it feels as if He's silent.

Other people function as if the Holy Spirit is in the background. While professing to believe in the power of the Holy Spirit, they trust in their own methodologies and personal strengths. In doing so, they deny the Holy Spirit and rely on the power and intellect of men. This is equally destructive. It forces men to look to themselves instead of God.

In each instance, the Holy Spirit is falsely accused. Since the Holy Spirit is a person, it grieves the Spirit when we sin against Him. We should desire a relationship with the Holy Spirit and learn the power that we have because of Him. To do so, God has given us His Word to guide us. In His Word, we learn that Christians are called to worship God in Spirit and truth. We'd do well to learn what this means.

To experience the Holy Spirit of God, we must draw near to Him in faith. In the next reading, we'll learn what it means to live a life of faith.

BIBLE PASSAGES

- **Ephesians 1:13** csb – 'In him you also were sealed with the promised Holy Spirit when you heard the word of truth, the gospel of your salvation, and when you believed.'

- **1 Corinthians 12:1-3** csb – 'Now concerning spiritual gifts: brothers and sisters, I do not want you to be unaware. You know that when you were pagans, you used to be enticed and led astray by mute idols. Therefore I want you to know that no one speaking by the Spirit of God says, "Jesus is cursed," and no one can say, "Jesus is Lord," except by the Holy Spirit.'

- **Joel 2:28** csb – 'After this I will pour out my Spirit on all humanity; then your sons and your daughters will prophesy, your old men will have dreams, and your young men will see visions.'

- **Ephesians 4:30** csb – 'And don't grieve God's Holy Spirit. You were sealed by him for the day of redemption.'

QUESTIONS FOR REFLECTION

1. Do you try to obey God by your own strength or by the power of the Holy Spirit?

2. Do you know how the Spirit has empowered you with spiritual gifts? Will you commit to discovering the gifts the Spirit has given you?

3. How does it make you feel knowing that the same Spirit who raised Jesus from the grave makes Himself available to Christians? Should you ever be afraid?

PRAYER

God, Holy Spirit, I want to know you more. Help me rely on the strength you give me and not on my own strength.

'God doesn't call us to be comfortable. He calls us to trust Him so completely that we are unafraid to put ourselves in situations where we will be in trouble if He doesn't come through.' – Francis Chan[1]

A People of Faith

If you're like me, you don't want to read about a powerful God. Instead, you want to see His power. What good is a God who's powerless? I'd say, 'Not good at all!' The Christian God is the only God, and He's full of power. His wisdom and power are evident in the things that have been made. Only a powerful being can speak into existence what you see around you. When you live by faith, and obediently trust God, you'll know His power personally. Christians are a people of faith.

The Bible teaches that 'faith is the reality of what is hoped for, the proof of what is not seen' (Heb. 11:1 CSB). This means the very presence of faith proves that God exists. I don't intend to say that all faith is equal. For example, belief in the Muslim god doesn't mean that he's real. Instead, I mean to say that the Christian God can be known by the power that His people possess.

The greatest power Christians have is our faith, and God promises to bless those who live by faith. Therefore, when you meet someone who has genuine faith in God, you'll see the proof of God displayed in his life by the ways that God blesses him. In the same way, the person who lives by faith will be convinced of God's existence by the power

1. Francis Chan, *Crazy Love* (Colorado Springs: David C. Cook, 2008).

that they possess and the experience they have with God. A person who lives by faith will know God personally. A person of faith is proof of the reality of God.

Faith gives us the power to *live* our walk with God. The Bible teaches 'without faith it is impossible to please God, since the one who draws near to him must believe that he exists and that he rewards those who seek him' (Heb. 11:6 CSB). So you see, if you believe in God, you'll live by faith because you believe that He's true. When you believe that God is real, you'll follow His commands, knowing that He rewards you when you do. Only those who live by faith will experience the rewards of God. In this way, you'll never know the goodness of God if you don't live by faith.

Those who doubt God and refuse to live by faith lack the power that exists in a faithful follower of Christ. They cannot please God since God requires His followers to trust Him in all circumstances. Why, is this important? Well, if you want to know God, you must live by faith, even when it's difficult.

Throughout history, the people of God have had a tendency to flirt with the world. At times, there's no way to identify a true Christian in a small crowd. It's become regular for the people of God to reject a lifestyle of faith in exchange for the ways of the world. As a result, they deny clear commands of Scripture to avoid rejection. Yet, the Bible teaches that Christians will not be accepted by the world because we don't belong to the world; we belong to God.

It's tempting to live by the standards of the world because the world doesn't require faith. The world gives you control. It tells you that you can determine the outcome of your life by the choices you make. Wasn't that the lie of Satan? To succeed in the world, you must become like the world, since the world only accepts its own.

Living by faith requires you to follow God and reject the ways of the world, even when it puts you in danger. When you live by faith, God gets to determine the outcome of your life; and by faith, you must submit to His choices. In doing so, you'll experience His power, protection, and provision. Living by faith isn't popular.

At times, what is said to be faith is actually foolishness. For example, living by faith doesn't mean that Christians become arrogant, lazy, or irresponsible members of society. Instead, it means we faithfully obey God and live as an example to the world. By rejecting the world, we tell the world that Jesus is good; that they no longer must be enslaved to the world and its devices. Unbelievers should know that God is good and real by observing your life.

Faith requires faithfulness. For this reason, we must trust God with the things He's entrusted to us. Some people are quick to change their plans as soon as things get difficult. Others become freeloaders and make excuses for their lack of commitment. They always claim that God is moving them on and will provide for their needs. In reality, remaining faithful in a difficult situation over many years often requires a great deal of faith.

Faith is obedience to God, according to His Word, no matter the outcome. Sometimes, when you trust God in faith, He'll part the sea in front of you. Other times, when you obey Him in faith, He'll miraculously provide for you. Many times, by faith, God will call you to obey Him in a world that is radically opposed to Him. In every instance, faith results in obedience out of a deep trust in God and His promises.

Christians that live by faith, rest in the promises of God. In the final reading, we'll discuss what it means to rest in God.

BIBLE PASSAGES

- *Hebrews 10:38* csb – 'But my righteous one will live by faith; and if he draws back, I have no pleasure in him.'

- *Hebrews 11:1-2* csb – 'Now faith is the reality of what is hoped for, the proof of what is not seen. For by it our ancestors won God's approval.'

- *Hebrews 11:6* csb – 'Now without faith it is impossible to please God, since the one who draws near to him must believe that he exists and that he rewards those who seek him.'

QUESTIONS FOR REFLECTION

1. Do you live by worldly wisdom or by faith in God? Do you trust God with all situations and events in your life, and are you ready and willing to obey Him no matter the cost?

2. Why should you trust God in all things? Why should you obey Him by faith?

3. Why is it important to be faithful to God with the things He's entrusted to your care?

PRAYER

God, you spoke all things into existence and sent your Son for my salvation. I can trust you in all things. Help me to live by faith and not by sight.

'You have made us for yourself, O Lord, and our hearts are restless until they find their rest in You.' – Augustine of Hippo[1]

A People of Rest

Last year, I totaled my car. I was making a left turn out of a parking lot, and a tree blocked my view. I thought it was clear, I crept out of the driveway, and a woman slammed into my door. Her car was also totaled. She struck me so hard that her entire front end was ruined. I'm shocked that I walked away with no injuries.

Now that I didn't have a car, I needed to find a way home. I was fasting that day and was shaken up. So, I decided to get something to eat. Once the police left, I walked to a coffee shop in the area. It was a fifteen-minute walk. During this time, I called my wife and asked her to pick me up. After we determined it was too complicated, I called a friend from church. He agreed to come, and started on his way.

As he began to drive, he saw that traffic was terrible. We happened to have a group at church that same night. Realizing that we'd be late if he came, he decided to call a rideshare. At first, I was hesitant to accept his help, but eventually agreed. The driver arrived, and we headed toward my destination.

Within minutes, the driver and I struck up a conversation. He asked how my day was going and I told him what had happened. After sharing a few more words, he began to talk to me about his life. He shared that he was struggling and that he'd had a rough few

---

1. Augustine of Hippo. *Confessions*. Book 1, Chapter 1.

months. His cousin had committed suicide – and he was anxious about his wife's pregnancy. I asked if I could pray for him, and to my surprise, he agreed. As soon as I had finished, his face lit up. I wasn't prepared for what he would say next.

The man was a follower of Christ. However, ever since his cousin had died, he had been struggling with marijuana use. His wife had asked him to quit, but he was overcome by addiction. He grieved the loss of his cousin – and marijuana helped him escape his feelings. Thirty minutes before I had gotten into the car, he had prayed to God. He had promised to throw away all of his marijuana if God were to put someone in his vehicle who would pray for him. I was blown away.

Instead of taking me home, we decided to meet my friends in a parking lot and pray for him. In the middle of the lot, he got on his knees, and we prayed. Following our prayer, he threw away his marijuana and decided to come to the group. When we arrived, the story got even more interesting.

As he was driving to the group, he called his wife and told her everything that had happened. Somehow, in their conversation, he realized that she knew me. In fact, a few months earlier, my mom had been involved in their wedding. God is deeply involved in the life of every Christian.

Let's recount the story: I got into an accident, walked fifteen minutes to a coffee shop, and then called my wife. After talking with her, we decided to ask a friend to pick me up. He began to drive, but then realized it would be faster to call a rideshare. Meanwhile, the husband of my mother's friend—a rideshare driver—was praying. He happened to be in the same area as I was. At the very moment the ride was requested, he was available. I got in the car, and the rest is history.

The Christian life is full of adventure, decision, and acts of obedience. There is joy, hardship, trial, and victory. Sometimes, God shares His plan with us; while other times, He requires us to obey Him when we can't see the outcome. In everything, Christians are a people of rest. Like the story above, we know that God is always working – even in tragedies. For this reason, Christians rest in God in all situations, whether those situations make sense or not. Christians are a people of rest.

As you complete this book, make a decision to rest in God. Choose to live for God in complete obedience. Join a church, read your Bible, and commit to the process of sanctification. Pursue an intimate relationship with Jesus. Tell your friends and family about Him. Stand up for justice and righteousness in the world and ask the Holy Spirit to guide you. In all things, remember that this world will fail you. Thankfully, God is building a new world – his coming Kingdom. Look forward to that world, and live accordingly. Be hopeful – God has overcome the world.

I pray that God will change your life like He's changed mine. I'm confident that He will.

BIBLE PASSAGES

- **Psalm 127:1-2** csb – *'Unless the Lord builds a house, its builders labor over it in vain; unless the Lord watches over a city, the watchman stays alert in vain. In vain you get up early and stay up late, working hard to have enough food – yes, he gives sleep to the one he loves.'*

- **Proverbs 16:9** csb – *'A person's heart plans his way, but the Lord determines his steps.'*

- **Matthew 11:28** csb – *'Come to me, all of you who are weary and burdened, and I will give you rest.'*

QUESTIONS FOR REFLECTION

1. Do you live in anxiety, or do you trust God with the outcome of your life? If someone assessed your life, would they believe that you trust God with the result of your life?

2. If God is in complete control of the outcome, should you ever worry? In this case, how should you organize your life, knowing that victory belongs to God?

3. How does it make you feel knowing that you don't have to be in control? Practically, what would it look like to release control? How would you make time to rest in and enjoy God?

PRAYER
Father, you are in control. Your plan is perfect, and your ways are right. Help me release control of my life and to entrust the outcome to you. Help me to rest in you.

Summary

In a short paragraph, summarize what you've learned in this chapter:

....

....

....

....

....

....

....

....

Questions

Write down any questions you would like to ask at your next meet-up:

....

....

....

....

....

....

....

....

Summary

In a short paragraph, summarize what you've learned in this chapter.

Questions

Write down any questions you would like to ask at your next meet-up:

'A farmer is helpless to grow grain; all he can do is provide the right conditions for the growing of grain. He cultivates the ground, he plants the seed, he waters the plants, and then the natural forces of the earth take over and up comes the grain. This is the way it is with Spiritual Disciplines – they are a way of sowing the Spirit. The Disciplines are God's way of getting us into the ground; they put us where He can work within us and transform us. By themselves the Spiritual Disciplines can do nothing; they can only get us to the place where something can be done. They are God's means of grace.' – Richard Foster[1]

Ten Spiritual Disciplines for the Christian Life

1. Prayer

- ***Philippians 4:6*** CSB – *'Don't worry about anything, but in everything, through prayer and petition with thanksgiving, present your requests to God.'*

Prayer is the act of communicating with God. In prayer, the believer acknowledges the magnificence of God, confesses sin, and thanks God for the many blessings He provides. He or she also asks God to meet his/her needs. This discipline is best practiced at regular intervals throughout the day and in special times of need. In prayer, power is found.

---

1. Richard J. Foster, *A Celebration of Discipline* (New York: HarperCollins, 1978, 1988, 1998), 7.

2. Silence and Meditation

- ***Matthew 6:7*** *csb* – *'When you pray, don't babble like the Gentiles, since they imagine they'll be heard for their many words.'*

In a busy and anxious world, the discipline of silence and meditation reminds the believer that God is in control. This discipline is best practiced in a quiet place over an extended period of time. During this time, a believer should meditate on God's Word, and listen for the quiet prompting of the Holy Spirit. Silence and meditation are a form of *listening* prayer.

3. Bible Reading

- ***Psalm 119:11*** *csb* – *'I have treasured your word in my heart so that I may not sin against you.'*

Bible reading is the act of seeking God as He's revealed Himself to us. By reading the Bible, the believer gets to know the true God. In doing so, the believer can also distinguish between the things that are true and of God versus and those things that are false. Christians should read their Bible daily and seek to obey what they learn.

4. Fasting

- ***Joel 2:12*** *csb* – *'Even now—this is the Lord's declaration—turn to me with all your heart, with fasting, weeping, and mourning.'*

Fasting is the intentional act of abstaining from food in order to focus the heart on God. Fasting reminds the believer that he or she is dependent upon God. By heightening our senses, fasting provides a unique opportunity to hear God's voice. This discipline is best practiced is special times of listening. It's important to note that biblical fasting is done for spiritual reasons and not for health reasons. Although it has become fashionable to fast from electronics or other worldly pleasures, biblical fasting is almost always the abstinence of food.

5. Stewardship

- *1 Peter 4:10* CSB – *'Just as each one has received a gift, use it to serve others, as good stewards of the varied grace of God.'*

Stewardship is an act of worship; one where the believer takes the resources and utilizes them for the glory of God. In this way, believers make a conscious decision to invest in God's Kingdom sacrificially. This includes financial investment, time investment, and the use of personal talents and abilities. It may also include opening their home or sharing their possessions. By doing so, the believer declares that all of life belongs to God.

6. Simplicity

- *Luke 12:15* CSB – *'He then told them, "Watch out and be on guard against all greed, because one's life is not in the abundance of his possessions".'*

The discipline of simplicity is the regular process of ensuring that no earthly attachments overshadow our joy in God. In this way, believers make a conscious effort to find their contentment in God alone. This does not mean that believers refrain from enjoying earthly pleasures, but instead that they maintain a proper relationship with them.

7. Fellowship

- *Hebrews 10:24-25* CSB – *'And let us watch out for one another to provoke love and good works, not neglecting to gather together, as some are in the habit of doing, but encouraging each other, and all the more as you see the day approaching.'*

Christians need each other. The act of fellowship provides the believer with the necessary support to follow God in this life. In Christian fellowship, the Holy Spirit works through each individual believer to strengthen the entire Body of Christ. There's no such thing as a Christian nomad; therefore, Christians must actively participate in Christian fellowship.

8. Confession

- *James 5:16* CSB – *'Therefore, confess your sins to one another and pray for one another, so that you may be healed. The prayer of a righteous person is very powerful in its effect.'*

Confession is the act of sharing your sins with God and with others. Secret sin will keep you in bondage. Christians experience the freedom of the Gospel when they encounter the grace of God in response to their sin. This discipline is best practiced in the confidence of mature Christians. Believers should confess all sin at all times.

9. Journaling

- *Psalm 119:15* CSB – *'I will meditate on your precepts and think about your ways.'*

Journaling is the act of documenting the works of God and of writing out your feelings of Him. In journaling, believers have the opportunity to trace their spiritual progress over the course of a lifetime. By doing so, the believer possesses a historical timeline of God's personal interaction with himself or herself.

10. Evangelism

- *Mark 16:15* CSB – *'Then he said to them, "Go into all the world and preach the gospel to all creation".'*

Evangelism is the act of sharing your faith with non-Christians. Through evangelism, God breaks the bonds of Satan in the world. Through evangelism, the believer gets to see the power of God in others.

Also available from Christian Focus Publications …

GOD
IS HE OUT THERE?

MEZ MCCONNELL

WAR
WHY DID LIFE JUST GET HARDER?

MEZ MCCONNELL

VOICES
WHO AM I LISTENING TO?

ANDY PRIME

BIBLE
CAN WE TRUST IT?

ANDREW MATHIESON

BELIEVE
WHAT SHOULD I KNOW?

MIKE MCKINLEY

 **9Marks**

First Steps series

The First Steps series will help equip those from an unchurched background take the first steps in following Jesus. We call this the 'pathway to service' as we believe that every Christian should be equipped to be of service to Christ and His church no matter your background or life experience.

If you are a church leader doing ministry in hard places, use these books as a tool to help grow those who are unfamiliar with the teachings of Jesus into new disciples. These books will equip them to grow in character, knowledge and action.

Or if you yourself are new to the Christian faith, still struggling to make sense of what a Christian is, or what the Bible actually says, then this is an easy to understand guide as you take your first steps as a follower of Jesus.

1. GOD: Is He Out There?

2. WAR: Why Did Life Just Get Harder?

3. VOICES: Who Am I Listening To?

4. BIBLE: Can We Trust It?

5. BELIEVE: What Should I Know?

6. CHARACTER: How Do I Change?

7. TRAINING: How Do I Live and Grow?

8. CHURCH: Do I Have To Go?

9. RELATIONSHIPS: How Do I Make Things Right?

10. SERVICE: How Do I Give Back?

Christian Focus Publications

Our mission statement —

STAYING FAITHFUL

In dependence upon God we seek to impact the world through literature faithful to His infallible Word, the Bible. Our aim is to ensure that the Lord Jesus Christ is presented as the only hope to obtain forgiveness of sin, live a useful life and look forward to heaven with Him.

Our books are published in four imprints:

CHRISTIAN
FOCUS

Popular works including biographies, commentaries, basic doctrine and Christian living.

CHRISTIAN
HERITAGE

Books representing some of the best material from the rich heritage of the church.

MENTOR

Books written at a level suitable for Bible College and seminary students, pastors, and other serious readers. The imprint includes commentaries, doctrinal studies, examination of current issues and church history.

CF4•K

Children's books for quality Bible teaching and for all age groups: Sunday school curriculum, puzzle and activity books; personal and family devotional titles, biographies and inspirational stories — because you are never too young to know Jesus!

Christian Focus Publications Ltd,
Geanies House, Fearn, Ross-shire,
IV20 1TW, Scotland, United Kingdom.
www.christianfocus.com
blog.christianfocus.com